Contents

Part I - The Chakras and Your Life

Chapter 1
Possibilities Open Up! 1
What is a Chakra?

Chapter 2
Living From Experience 7
The Ego Belief System
The Ego System
The Ego
Perceptions
Fully Living the Experience
Living From Expression

Chapter 3
Spiritual Principles 17
Detachment - Desire, Not Need
Non-Judgment - No Value System, Discernment
Now-Moment - The Point of Power
Intent

Part II - The Seven Major Chakras

Experiencing Life Through The Chakras

How The Chakras Affect Your
Decisions, Success, and Perspective on Life

Based on the Teachings of

Salem

Through
Diandra

By Clarence Deigel

A Book in the Path To Remembrance Series

Clarmar Publishing
Lincolnshire, Il. 60069

Experiencing Life Through The Chakras
How the Chakras Affect Your Decisions, Success and Perspective on Life
by Clarence Deigel

Published By:
Clarmar Publishing
A Division of Clarmar LLC
P.O. Box 619
Lincolnshire, Il. 60069-0619
Orders@ClarmarPublishing.com
http://www.ClarmarPublishing.com

For information, contact *Clarmar Publishing*

Library of Congress Control Number: 2003090748

ISBN, print ed. softcover   0-9722680-3-0
First Printing 2003

Disclaimer

This book provides information on the chakra system that is meant to inform, educate and presents a point of view for your discernment or thought. It is sold with the understanding that the publisher and author neither gives medical advice nor prescribes techniques as a form of treatment, either directly or indirectly for physical, mental, or medical problems. The information in this book is not to be construed as a substitute for professional medical treatment or advice. Any action that the reader takes with respect to the information in this book is at the reader's discretion, and the author or publisher assumes no responsibility for the actions of the reader.

In Appreciation

My heartfelt thanks to my wife Margaret, for her love, believing in me, encouraging me, and her steadfast support in enduring the long hours necessary to produce this book. For all of those reasons and more, she has played a great role in making this book a reality.

To Diandra for her trust and support of my efforts in bringing Salem's teachings to others so they may benefit, and for her many hours of reading the various revisions and her many thoughtful suggestions. Thank you!

My thanks to the universe for Diandra's special ability in bringing Salem's message to the planet.

To Diandra's husband, Batavia, for his many suggestions and generous help with the technical aspects of the book, and for his unwavering support and belief in the message Diandra brings forth.

My great appreciation to the weekly discussion group that has been a fertile ground for my growth and a testament to how Salem's message can open possibilities in peoples lives. To Linda Ewing, Bernadette Hughes, Marie Krag, Christina Lurski, Burt & Lou Von Ohlen, Shirley Skillin, and Karin Stenaae, I appreciate your sincerity, support and thank you for the love you send to the world.

My deep gratitude to Donna Wozniak who has spent many hours editing this manuscript, and for her many suggestions!

A special thank you to Salem for his teachings and unwavering unconditional love for humanity and the planet.

I would like to acknowledge all of the souls who have spoken their truth while living on the planet. Their sharing has formed a foundation from which the consciousness of the planet has and continues to expand.

Finally, special thanks to Nell Daniel for her love, guidance, and understanding, which has been instrumental to my spiritual growth in this life.

Preface

You may think, "What, another book about the Chakras!" Knowledge about the chakras has been on the planet for thousands of years. In recent years, this knowledge and the topic of the chakras have spawned the writing of many books in the western world. So why another one; hasn't it all been covered?

Much has been written about how the chakras relate to the various organs and how the chakras can effect the healing of the physical body. That is not the primary focus of this book. Salem's teachings address the chakras from a different perspective with the emphasis on how the chakras affect the way you experience and process your everyday life, and how working with the chakra system can help to liberate oneself from self-imposed limitations that have long been forgotten.

Yes, working with the chakra system can help heal the physical body, for the body is only an outward reflection of what is within and what is within is directly related to the chakras. But it is how we "experience the experience" in our daily lives that ultimately affects not only the physical body, but the choices we make in life, and what we feel safe enough to pursue in our lives.

We live on a freewill planet and though that freewill would never be violated, there is much Love in the Universe for humanity. From that Love, "ways" have been made available to help humanity on its spiritual path. Of course, it is always left to the individual and humanity to choose to make use of this help. The methods and techniques described in this book enable you to tap into these "ways" to make working with your chakras easy and without a great deal of work. Using these techniques and methods can help you to easily clear blockages accumulated from your life's experiences allowing new possibilities to open in your life.

We live in an age where information is readily available. Information is for the analytical aspects of the mind, and although important, it not always translates into something that you can do or experience to help reach your goals. The techniques given to work with your chakra system can be used and experienced everyday (rather than just information to be processed by the mind) to help you on your spiritual journey.

The chakra system can play a vital role in helping to free you from self-imposed limitations and open new possibilities in your life. Therefore, working with the chakra system can be an important and beneficial endeavor on your path to remembrance and the discovery of who you really are. For all of these reasons and more, another book on the topic seemed worth the effort to make this information available for the benefit of all whom read it.

At this point you may be wondering, "Who is Salem"? To help answer that question, a section has been included ("Who is Salem: A message from Salem") allowing Salem to tell about himself. In the simplest terms, Salem is an entity that communicates through Diandra, and although that may not be the usual manner for information to be introduced to the world, it is one that has some distinct advantages. The biggest advantage is perspective. Salem brings a perspective that is outside and not hampered by being immersed in the physical, allowing fresh and new views about life and humanity to be introduced.

You may also wonder how you can know that the information given in this book is valid, for it does not easily hold up to such obvious means of validation, as say, dropping an apple to verify the existence of gravity. That kind of proof shall not be attempted in this book; rather the information shall be allowed to stand on its own for you to decide its merits. But if you agree that the possibility exists that we are more than what we know and understand ourselves to be, then it may be reasonable to think that the "more" may not be revealed through the same familiar methods, means, and thinking patterns that we have come to know. To go beyond what we know will likely take other methods and means. I believe Salem gives us another method and means to help us once again become more by understanding, remembering and rediscovering our potentials of who we really are. To the extent that is true, will depend on how Salem's teachings speak to your inner knowing and truth, and ultimately how that shows up in your life. That is the proof. To the extent that it does show up in your life will depend upon how much you trust your inner knowing and truth, and that is only for you to decide.

Note to the Reader

This is an exciting time to be on the planet. The planet is in transition. Much is in a state of flux in which the energies are no longer as fixed. This is an opportunity to reconstruct these energies in a manner that will promote Love and healing.

Healing of the planet or anything always begins with oneself. In order to facilitate the healing and reconstruction, it is necessary that you are able to stay centered and in your power. Clearing your chakras is a powerful tool that can help you to center in the power that you are and discover the unlimited possibilties of your creative existence. This book is dedicated to helping all who desire to nurture themselves and the planet by being a source of light and Love for the world.

Clarence Deigel

About the Author

Like many, the journey of my life has been propelled from a yearning within to understand some of life's deeper questions. In the beginning, this yearning was driven from a dissatisfaction with the answers commonly given leading to a search both within and without for answers and understanding. This quest has taken me on a journey of both the spiritual and scientific sides of life. At times the answers I found were not something that could be comprehended by the mind, but rather experienced by treading into waters the mind was not always comfortable with, stretching past my comfort zone, and being brave enough to follow the nudges from within. I am sure many have followed their yearnings from within in guiding their lives to express all that they are.

I have spent many years of my adult life exploring the spiritual aspect of existence allowing my inner guide to lead the way. As I explored both sides of the question, my search included receiving a degree in physics from a Midwestern university and spending over twenty years working as an engineer and manager for a fortune 500 company. I currently live in the Chicago area with my wife Margaret and prior to that I lived in Europe and various places around the United States.

I now devote a large portion of my energies making information available through books, seminars, and discussion groups. The website http://www.PathToRemembrance.com is dedicated to being an online resource to assist others on their spiritual journey. It is my hope the message, methods and techniques embodied in the material presented can help others on their spiritual paths and further the expansion of consciousness and self-awareness on the planet.

Over the last several years I have led seminars and discussion groups with emphasis on the Salem message. The teachings of Salem have fit very well with my truth and all I have encountered on my spiritual journey. I am currently working on a book that will bring together a large portion of Salem's message and will be part of *The Path To Remembrance* series of works.

I have known and worked with Diandra since 1994. During this time our friendship and respect for each other has grown. I am thankful and honored for Diandra's support in allowing me to play a part in helping to bring the Salem message to others.

About Diandra

Diandra is an internationally-known spiritual teacher, retreat leader and personal consultant. In 1986 Diandra left a successful career in finance to dedicate her life to full-time spiritual service. In 1993 Diandra and her soul mate, Batavia co-founded Inward Journey – Gateway to Expansion, an organization dedicated to helping others find and live their inner truths. Inward Journey maintains a base in both the Midwest and the Southwest part of the United States.

Diandra joins with others in this organization to bring the message of remembrance that we are Love. Those whose lives she touches feel her love for others, this planet, and all life.

Diandra spent much of her younger life with missionary grandparents under whose guidance she developed a deep relationship with the spiritual essence of life. This spiritual awareness would prepare her for her life today.

In 1980 Diandra was involved in an automobile accident that left her in bed with a back injury for fourteen months. During that time, her constant search was for a deeper understanding of God, truth and the meaning of life. This search led to months of prayer, meditation and continuous questions to the Creator.

Diandra spent long hours asking the deep questions of the meaning of life and wrote her answers in a journal. Slowly she began to realize this knowledge was from a source with greater awareness than her. When she asked where this information was coming from, the answer was Salem. Since that time Salem has shared many truths giving great guidance for a better way of life on this planet.

Diandra is author of the book *A New Day Is Dawning* (available at your local bookstore or from the Inward Journey website). She is a frequent contributor to the "Sedona Journal" and the Internet site "Spirit Web" as well as numerous other publications.

Diandra is available for personal consultations either in person or by phone. Having over twenty years of consulting experience, she gives clients insight into important issues affecting their lives. Diandra has helped thousands of people all over the world gain clarity, direction and purpose in their lives. Clients consistently comment on the accuracy, professionalism and empowering nature of Diandra's consultations.

Diandra can be reached for an appointment at:

1-800-578-8090
Credit cards are welcome

Audio tapes of Salem's messages on a wide variety of topics are also offered at the Inward Journey website:

http://www.inwardjourney.com.

Who Is Salem
A Message From Salem

My friends, I am you and you are me. I am a state of consciousness. No, I have never incarnated on your planet. I identify myself as an ambassador to many universes or levels of consciousness, for my consciousness is not embodied in one level of understanding but has chosen to move through many levels of consciousness. With great delight my consciousness travels through these levels or universes, for they are filled with wonder. I never travel those journeys that I do not expand, grow, or become more self-aware. The most spectacular part of my soul's journey is the beauty I see in all levels of consciousness for all is Divine creation and all has beauty.

I know nothing that you do not already know. I express nothing that you cannot express. I am simply an individualized expression as are you, united in a group consciousness that extends a great amount of love to your planet. I am part of a totality of consciousness that expresses, much as others of love you have known are part of a consciousness that expresses.

Because I have awareness of many levels of consciousness, I am able to bring a "clarity of information" without being subjective. The consciousness I represent has a great clarity of pragmatic knowledge of experience, expression, time and space that can be of benefit to you. Together we choose to share this "clarity of information" with you to help in whatever way we can. We feel just our presence within your universe can help you to open and expand to other levels of consciousness existing within you even if we never spoke a word to you.

We are not about how smart or evolved we can become. We are not about being a higher consciousness from others or concerned there is a higher consciousness from us. It does not exist for us. To us, all creations are magnificent and a delight to observe, explore, and commune with because we truly connect with the beauty of all life.

What you might consider to be the most insignificant, smallest life form on the planet is magnificent. We can observe one little insect and marvel at the intelligence, instincts and the self-awareness of this life form. We watch this life form as it maneuvers through life at its level of consciousness and recognize that it is beautiful and wonderful.

We live in the beauty of the consciousness of All-That-Is. Is that not what you desire to do? You miss so many beautiful things in your world because you have judged them to be unsafe. You either fear them, think they can harm you or they are an annoyance, but in actuality they are beautiful and wondrous, and we would encourage you to look for the beauty that exists in your world. As we speak to you, it is only to try to help you awaken to the wonder and the beauty of who you are: the beauty of life, the beauty of existence, and the sacredness of All-That-Is.

We recognize you have imprisoned yourselves in your belief system, for that is all it is, your belief. As you begin to change your beliefs, you will change, but how can you change when what you believe seems so real to you? We recognize it is not real, and just our connecting with you brings a vibration of reality, a clarity helping you to move into that reality yourself.

You might wonder why is it that I speak through Diandra? This has been an ongoing agreement and collaboration for many lifetimes. So it is easy for me to express through this particular personality. I have chosen to be a spokesperson through this particular vehicle to help you realize the truth lying within you.

I am merely a friend that is here to help you obtain a greater clarity of who you are, and to see your beautiful planet become the totality of your expression. Your soul expression within the physical dimension is the crowning jewel of creation and because of that in many ways you are much more than I.

If we could take you through the universal consciousness, the halls of experience and expression, we would do that, but you must journey there yourself. We cannot because we would not and cannot interfere with your freewill. It is your choice to allow your consciousness to expand or not. Anything we can say to help you to awaken is our mission and our purpose. Ask for our help. We can help you, but you must ask. Ask the angels for help. They are there to help you.

We are you and you are we. We certainly are no greater than you. We are all one, the sacredness of existence, life and beauty. It is our awareness of that sacredness that brings us together. As you become aware and expand, so do we. We love you unconditionally because you exist, and we see all of the beauty and awareness that you are... and I am Salem.

Part I

The Chakras and Your Life

"It is not what is happening in your life that matters but rather how you are experiencing the experience."

Salem

1
****

POSSIBILITIES OPEN UP!

The purpose of this book is to help you open your life's possibilities through understanding and working with your chakra system. The chapters that follow will explain what the chakras are, how the chakras affect your life, and how to work with the chakra system to clear away lifetimes of blockages that limit your life's possibilities.

Presently, when you think of what you desire, you focus and begin to create from a process that utilizes clogged chakras that limit your creative choices. Before your mind has a chance to analyze, or the subconscious has a chance to decide, the chakra system has already eliminated thousands of possibilities for you. You may think your desires to be impossible because past experience has said they are impossible, they have not worked, or they have not happened before. Consequently, your desires do not even become a possibility for you to consider or make a decision upon.

When your chakras are clear, they no longer block your creativity. What you once considered to be impossible becomes probable. You are not as bound by past experiences, or as afraid to pursue opportunities and the things you desire to do in your life. You are no longer limited by the fear within the chakras. Therefore, you begin to feel lighter and think in terms of possibilities being realities where before they were impossibilities or only vague possibilities. Your life opens up, and you discover there are more possibilities to consider and choose from in your life. You begin to see the expansiveness of life because you do not perceive experiences from a narrow, focused point of view. You expand and connect in a more powerful way with the higher portions of yourself, and you begin to see and perceive beauty in every moment of your life.

All of these things can be an expansion that takes place within you, but you have to decide if you want to live and create in a much larger playing field from what you have been living in for many lifetimes. Do you really want to take responsibility for your creative power? Do you really want to come from the essence of being unlimited?

Understanding, and working with your chakras can be a powerful, and rewarding endeavor that can expand your awareness and open the possibilities in your life.

What Is a Chakra?

At this point, you may be wondering, "What is a chakra?" The knowledge of chakras has been around the eastern part of the world for thousands of years. The practice of yoga embellishes the chakras and so the chakras are not new to the planet.

Chakra is a Sanskrit word meaning "wheel" or "vortex". The ancient Hindus defined chakras as a spinning wheel or energy center where the consciousness governing various physical and spiritual aspects resides. The Hindus determined that there are seven energy centers or wheels spinning in a clockwise direction, each having a different color. The chakras are part of what is referred to as the "subtle anatomy" (more about this in chapter four) with five chakras aligned along the spine and two in the head area as one would think of the physical body. They are: the red base/survival chakra, the orange sexual/creativity chakra, the yellow emotional/solar plexus chakra, the green heart/love chakra, the blue throat/will chakra, the indigo third-eye/vision chakra and the violet spiritual center or crown chakra (see figure 1).

The survival or base chakra resides at the base of the spine and connects or grounds you to the Earth. The Chakra at the opposite end, the spiritual or crown chakra is partly outside the physical body and connects to the spiritual essence. The placement of the chakras is thought to align with the major nerve or endocrine centers within the body.

The chakras are not physical and may be more appropriately thought of as aspects of consciousness. Salem refers to the chakras as energy centers that define various aspects of experience within the physical. Since consciousness can be equated in simple terms to awareness, you could think of the chakras as centers of awareness or aspects of consciousness that define both physical and spiritual attributes of experience within the physical.

To fully appreciate this view of the chakras it is necessary to lay some groundwork before going into the heart of the chakra system. The next few chapters of this book will lay this groundwork.

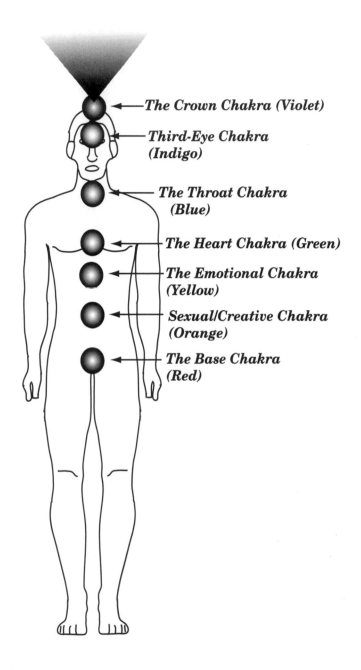

Figure 1
The Chakra System

2

✳✳✳✳✳✳✳

LIVING FROM EXPERIENCE

To fully understand and appreciate how the chakra system affects your life we shall start by examining how you process life. If you think about it, your world is simply a compilation of experiences. Experience is how you live life. If experience says it is so, it is so. If experience says it is not so, you find difficulty in believing how other possibilities can become an experience in your life. So how did this view and belief about life come about?

The Ego Belief System

As you journey on the planet, with your soul being housed within your physical body and your Spirit at the helm attempting to guide you, the greatest challenge for humanity is the ego belief system.

The ego belief system has at its core a belief in separation.

There came a point in the evolution of humanity within the physical where the thought came about that physical was a self-contained existence separate from the Creator and other dimensions or levels of existence. Once that belief was accepted, it seeded the belief that physical existence could be threatening and one could be destroyed. You then became entrapped because you believed you were no longer connected to Divinity, which said you were an unlimited being and one with everything. This system of beliefs spawned from the belief in separation is what is called the ego belief system.

The ego belief system believes everything you are not and is totally unaware of the truth, the totality and the reality of who you truly are.

The ego belief system is embedded within the mass consciousness. Even if in your heart and soul you understand you are more than what you know, you are one with all life, God expressing, all things are possible to you, and you are the creator of your reality, you are still living with the influence of an individual, physical body appearing to be separate from all things having its own vulnerabilities. You, therefore, at times feel threatened, lonely or powerless. This is the ego system you have marvelously created in your own defense from the need to feel safe.

The Ego System

The self, through its evolution within the physical dimension, has developed a system of survival, the ego system. The ego system is not about your philosophy or psychology of who you are but instead about the system you created once you believed you were separate from the power the Creator had given to you.

The ego system was devised in order to keep a self that believes in limitation, safe. The need for safety came about because the ego became lost in the creations of the self and no longer understood its position as being a part of a self that is a creator. This is what is termed being disconnected from the source (separation) and is at the heart of your spiritual journey. You are at a time where many are finding their way back, expanding their consciousnesses and realizing they are creators of their world, souls expressing.

The ego system is based on the belief that you are separate from the Creator. In that belief, you created many elaborate defense systems to ensure your safety that together make up the ego system. Let's take a look at some of these systems.

As you began to develop the ego system, you moved from the Divine Mind, which knew everything, into an analytical mind to analyze your experiences. Now one of the prime purposes of the analytical mind is to analyze experience in a linear framework of time to determine if you are safe. Through this determining process, judgments are made and perceptions are formed.

Also as part of the design of the ego system, it was desired that a first line of defense would come into play even before the mind. This first line of defense is the emotions. The emotions fire up immediately to tell you if your safety is being threatened. In this context, the emotions are your most powerful creation, for you depend the most upon the emotions to stay safe.

The ego system is not the ego but a system devised by the self and used by the ego in order to assure safety.

The Ego

The ego belief system and ego system should not be confused with the ego. The ego is simply the outer most portion of the self that directly deals with life in the physical. It is the self that you think of as yourself. The ego is merely a portion of the self that is immersed in the physical and in that context is not limiting. But how the ego chooses to believe, view and use its abilities can be limiting.

The ego today views the world through your limited perceptions, fear-based opinions and limited knowledge of who you are.

In summary, the ego system consists of an analytical mind and an emotional system to help you stay safe based on a belief of being separate from the Creator and Divinity. The ego system serves the self very well in performing this function, but it is limiting.

Perceptions

As you began to live from the ego system, you began to live from the perception of your experiences. Everything your conscious mind is aware of is an experienced event, be that a conversation you are having, a catastrophe, the death of a friend, the birth of a new child, or a romantic encounter, etc. Whatever it might be, your interaction with these experiences is primarily from your perception rather than from the experience itself.

Perceptions have become the basis for the evaluation of your existence. Perceptions are simply the result of your ego system's analysis of how a past or similar experience has affected you. If you could have a totally new experience, meaning there were no experiences in your past that relate to the new experience, then you would not have any preconceived ideas or "perceptions" about this new experience. You would be free to fully live the new experience.

Two people can participate in the same event, but it is unlikely their perceptions of the event will be the same. There can be more differences in how the event is perceived than similarities. An example of this is two people skydive for the first time. One of the skydivers is excited and thrilled by the experience, the other dies of a heart attack. The normal, analytical mind question is what caused the death of the skydiver? As has been previously stated, the analytical mind always requires a cause and effect analysis so that perceptions of experiences can be formed and safety determined. The answer normally put forth is that jumping out of the plane caused the death of the skydiver; that is the cause. However, one could also conclude that it was the perception of the experience.

Both skydivers had the same experience, jumping out of the plane. One skydiver was enlivened by the experience; the other skydiver was literally frightened to death. Admittedly this may be an over simplified example, but it does demonstrate the importance of perception on our lives.

Another example that may help clarify how perceptions affect our lives is viewing an ax in a museum. The ax itself is very benign or dormant lying in the display case of the museum. But if the ax had motion, it could be dangerous and very frightening. This perception of the ax for some can create fear even though it is lying harmlessly within the display case.

Likewise the fear of heights is caused by the perception that one may fall and even die from the fall. This perception of heights can create great fear and anxiety from just thinking about heights. The fear of heights can cause people to freeze, and have very noticeable changes in body function: sweating, raised pulse rate, elevated blood pressure, etc. Yet there are many who do not have this fear allowing them to help build skyscrapers or in some instances climb them for fun. It is not the height that is cause of the fear but the perception of height that is limiting.

It is what you bring to the experience in the form of your perceptions that affects your life.

Your perceptions have placed limitations upon your life and for that reason you live from the perception of your experiences, not the experiences itself. An experience is simply an event. It is your perception of the event that determines how your survival and safety are affected.

Fully Living The Experience

Rather than living the experiences of your life from perceptions that are limiting, take a few moments to reflect upon fully living the experience.

To fully live the experience means to consciously feel the experience, expand into the experience, and unite with the experience without any restrictions. Become one with the experience without perception.

No matter how the experience may seem to your conscious mind, know everything in the experience is of benefit to you. You probably can think back to an experience that seemed difficult based on your perceptions, and in actuality it worked for your benefit.

You are the creator of your experiences. The more you can remove the perceptions that determine how you experience life, the less confusion and more clarity you will have and the more you will live and benefit on a conscious level from your experiences. Creativity will expand, and you will believe in the possibilities of your creative powers. You will begin to live the life you desire in the true rich abundance of experience.

By choosing to take the action of fully living your experiences everyday, you will find totally living an experience is fun and brings joy where perhaps there was none. You will begin to see things in a new light that will allow you to expand more into who you are.

It all begins with perception. As you perceive it, so you live it. Your perceptions are the determining factor of how you are living your life. The more you begin to live in the rich abundance of the experience and not from the perception, the more you will begin to use your expressive powers.

Living From Expression

As you have journeyed through your lifetimes on the planet, you have compiled many experiences. Your world has become a world of experience. Experiences have become your reality to such an extent that you no longer understand how to exist outside of experience. To live outside of experience means to take the next step and live from expression.

You were created to live as an expression of Divinity knowing no limits. You are an expression of Divinity. If you can let go of your perceptions of your experiences, you can evolve to the next step, which is expression.

Expression simply means you experience without limitation.

It is still a world of experience. Expression is living in the fullness of the experience without judgment, without attachments, without need, and in the power of the now-moment. To live in expression instead of from the limitation of perceptions of an experience is a giant leap. You live your existence as an experience in a richer, fuller manner, not from limitation, fear, pain, or emotions. To express is to live outside of the ego system without the perceptions of past experiences influencing your present experiences. In short, when you live from expression, your experiences do not determine your life. That means you are free to use your creative powers to express what is inside of you.

When you have a desire that comes from within, instead of analyzing it, trying to determine if it is feasible or not, you will know you have the ability to express this desire through your creative powers. You will not shut down the desire because the analytical mind has not figured out how to bring it about. When you shut down your desires, you block your creative powers, thereby, preventing your ability to express and fully live, and the life within you diminishes.

Fully living the experience is about "experiencing your experiences" without your perceptions coloring or distorting the experience. Living from expression is living and creating without limitation. You always create. It is a matter of whether your creations are the expression of what is within or determined by the constraints of your perceptions of what you have experienced.

3

****

SPIRITUAL PRINCIPLES

In the last chapter it was stated that living from expression is fully living the experience without attachments, judgments, and in the power of the now-moment. These are spiritual principles that can help you live your life without limitation and allow you to move into expression. In this chapter, these principles will be briefly explored.

Detachment – Desire, Not Need

In order for you to be free, the Principal of Detachment is mandatory. As long as you have an attachment to anything, a circumstance, your past, a person, or a need of any type, you will be subservient to the attachment. In a subservient position, you are neither free nor living from the seat of your power.

How do you recognize if you have attachments in your life? Look for things that you consider you need. If you must have a particular outcome to a situation, you have a need. If you feel your safety or happiness will be compromised when a particular outcome is not achieved, you have a need.

When you have an attachment, the need for feeling safe will motivate you to find ways to take control of the situation. The only thing you know to do is to control or manipulate the outcome if possible. If you are not attempting to control or manipulate the situation either subtly or overtly, you may still experience stress through worry or fear about the outcome. When you become aware of your attachments, you may be amazed at the amount of energy expended in maintaining your safety through your attachments.

You may think, "If I cannot need something, then what?" Instead of needing with a strong interest in an outcome, you can instead desire. Desires are different from needs. Desires are things you recognize you would enjoy and therefore propel you forward into a new experience. Desires help you to create a rich, full existence for yourself and your world but...

Desires never depend upon anything.

A desire will never depend upon interacting with another person or a situation occurring in a certain way. A desire will propel the energy forward and create in perfect harmony the very best for you. It is a far superior experience to that of attachment and need. However, until you feel safe enough to let go of your attachments and needs, you cannot come from the power of desire.

Non-Judgment – No Value System, Discernment

Judgment is placing a value system on your experiences. Judgments come from your perceptions of experiences. An experience is an experience; that is all it is. It is simply a happening, an event. However, your perception of the experience empowers it. If you perceive an experience to be enriching, positive, and one that enhances the quality of your life, then you are happy and therefore will judge (value) the experience as good. Likewise, if you perceive the same experience to threaten your safety in any way, then fear will rise up, and the perception will begin to limit you. You will then judge (value) the experience as bad. It does not take much thought to realize you place values (judgments) on many of your experiences. Besides judging your personal experiences, you also judge other people, events, situations, and circumstances that appear not to directly affect you.

The perceptions of your experiences dictate how you live and the prison you have created for yourself. As long as you have a need to judge, you shall always be imprisoned. Every time you hold a judgment of an experience, a person, or any event, you feed energy that keeps the imprisonment in place not only for yourself but also for the particular arena of the experience, the person, or situation.

When you judge another, it is only a reflection of what is inside of you. Your judgments do nothing but energize, empower, and hold in place what is inside of you.

Practicing non-judgment is not just being a Good Samaritan, for judgments imprison the one who judges as well.

If you cannot embrace and Love everything as it is, because it exists, then neutralize your energy and what you feed to it by not judging.

If you choose not to judge, what can you do? You can discern. Just as there is a difference between need and desire, there is a difference between judgment and discernment. You have created a brilliant mind capable of discerning very well. You can discern a situation or circumstance for what it is. There is nothing wrong with that. You can even choose to be part of an experience or not but do not judge by placing a value on it. Judgment says it is good or bad, right or wrong. You do not have to place a value on a situation, circumstance, or person in order to discern or to choose one thing versus another.

Perception and observing are two different things. Perception is laden with judgment. To observe an experience choosing to be a part of the experience or not is choice, and choice is not perception. You see if you do not perceive and you do not judge, you do not feed the experience. Your creative abilities are then not limited by your judgments and perceptions, and you are free to continually create whatever you desire in your world.

What you find is judgment and perceptions are circular whereby perceptions create judgments and judgments create perceptions. Thus, it is difficult to have one without the other.

But if you decide you will not make a judgment, then you will not create a perception that is limiting.

There is no good or bad— there just is!

Now-Moment – The Point of Power

The next spiritual principal is to move into the now-moment. That is what eternity is. Eternity is eternally the now-moment. There is no past, and there is no future in reality. Everything you create is created now. This does not mean you suddenly close your mind down and have no remembrance of events of the past or you do not plan for future events. It does mean you stay in the power of the now-moment. So how do you do that?

When you think of the past, and there are things that still trigger emotions in you, anger, frustration, regrets, etc., then those are still limiting you. Your past is still limiting you. Wrap the experience, the person, or the emotions in unconditional love, and in your mind bring them into the now-moment. Do not see it as in the past because it certainly is not. Those things are limiting and affecting you now! Bring them into the now-moment and Love them.

Wrap them in unconditional love or the God Consciousness of Love, and release them to become part of your creative power rather than your limitation.

Now what about the future? How do you bring the future into the now-moment? You do it by being excited about the future now. Do not live by being attached to future outcomes using your energy to control and manipulate those outcomes. Instead, be excited about your desires going forth, knowing they are going to be fulfilled.

When you *know* your desires are going to be fulfilled, you are not concerned about the outcome and therefore do not have to force a result through control or manipulation. Likewise, when you *know* your desires will be fulfilled, you do not need to set the parameters or the manner in which the fulfillment of the desire will come about. Your soul, Spirit, and the universal consciousness have a far better view of how to bring about your desires than your conscious, analytical mind. You live *now* with an excitement about the future and for your desires but not expecting so and so to do such and such to make your desires happen. Living in the now-moment does not mean to not plan nor set goals, but instead allow your greater consciousness and the universe to determine how to fulfill your desires. This is coming from the Divine mind instead of the ego or analytical mind.

Intent

Intent is not normally considered to be on the level of a spiritual principle, but it is a principle of importance and power just the same. Intent plays a vital role in working with the chakra system, and so a discussion of this principle is included in this chapter on spiritual principles.

The sequence of events that leads from a thought to a creation starts by setting intent and ends with surrender and trust.

Intent resonates within the universe activating your creative power and your ability to manifest your desires.

Intent comes only from your mental, emotional, or physical aspects—not from the spiritual, for the spiritual is what you are. Spiritual allows you to express and experience, but it has no intent.

Intent does not always require a deep focus in which you meditate and become very direct, although that will have a greater affect in manifesting your desires. Intent can simply be deciding to walk into a room and pick up a book. Your body responds to that intent set in motion by your thoughts.

Intent must begin with a thought. When you have a thought, you are activating the intent. The thought may be in response to a desire, a wish, a thought about someone, or a thought that is ego driven such as an emotion, but it is the beginning of the intent. Now all of your third-dimensional self, the emotions, your mind, and your physical will respond to the intent.

When you set the intent, be very single minded, do not sway because you send mixed messages to the universe: "I intend to see Aunt Sally, but I should really stay home today and clean the house." Well, what do you intend to do? Be single focused so your intent can be honored and empowered. Intents work best when they are single focused, and you know and trust that the universe will respond. It is a process, the creative process, so set the intent, trust the intent, and trust the universe will respond.

How does intention differ from desire? Desire is an energy that will begin to put things into motion. Desire will open doors for you, but unless you set the intent to go through the door, the desire may not manifest. You will find an excuse why you cannot fulfill your desire. Therefore, when you have a desire, also set your intent to fulfill the desire.

For instance, you may desire to take a trip around the world. Setting the intent to take a trip around the world does not mean you have to plan every little nuance of the trip, but set your intent to go around the world by some date. This is your desire and your intention. Set aside the vacation time, decide your wardrobe, begin to decide how you want to make the trip, etc. Now you have desire, intent, and action. Once you do this, everything begins to respond to your desire and intent. Your creative process becomes empowered, and the next thing you know you have a manifestation.

Intent is the activator behind your desires and choices. When something feels good, feels right, and it is something you like to do, then it is a desire and not a need. A desire is a positive motivator to an action. A choice may be made because of a perceived need or a choice may be made because of a desire or a need. For instance, "I desire to live on the coast, but I need to stay here because this is where my job is." A choice can be between two desires, a desire and a need, or between two needs. Desires will flow in harmony because they are of the soul and will not have the conflict that can occur between desire and need or between two needs.

Intent has become a weak link in the manifestation process, and we are not talking about the intent to get a drink of water. It is, therefore, important to remember that desire and need motivates, choice determines, but intent activates. If you want to activate something that is going to take a tremendous amount of creativity to come about, then the intent must have strong activation. You cannot say, "You know I think maybe I will intend to..." well that is not intent. That is a weak, wishy-washy, maybe I will maybe I won't. You have not intended anything. Maybe I will go to the post office today or maybe I will... now you are in a choice state and are not intending anything.

For example, you have set the intent to build a doghouse. The intent has to be strong enough to be the activator to obtain the material for the doghouse. If the intent is not that strong, then you procrastinate. Have you ever really wanted to do something badly? Now you really have a strong desire that is the motivator. This desire flows into the intent activating with the same strength and quickly you make it happen. Even if there are obstacles, you will find your way through them and make it happen, but without the activation of intent nothing happens. You can wish about it, you can think about it, you can dream about it, but unless you intend it to be, it does not come about. Intent is the activator!

4

****

YOUR VIBRATIONAL PATTERN

To this point we have explored how the ego system came into existence and the role it plays in determining how you process life through your experiences and perceptions, and how you interpret your experiences through perceptions that can limit you from truly expressing all that you are. Spiritual principles were also introduced that can help you begin to live your life from expression, allowing you to live life more fully and without limitation. With this groundwork laid, it is now time to explore how the chakras fit into your life.

In chapter one, a common definition of chakras was given as a wheel of spinning energy, where consciousness resides governing various attributes of individual physical and spiritual aspects. To many, a wheel of spinning energy or an energy center where consciousness resides is not a very tangible thing but neither are the emotions if you think about it. While there is no problem accepting the validity of the emotions, one could ask: Where are the emotions located? We accept the validity of the emotions because we feel their effects and likewise the effects of our perceptions are just as real. But where are the perceptions located? To help answer these questions and give some structure for the mind requires looking more into the essence of what we are.

You Are An Energy Or Vibrational Pattern

You are an energy or vibrational pattern that is all you are. Everything is energy vibrating or energy in motion. Energy in motion vibrates forming a unique pattern resulting in a creation whether that is tangible or intangible. The resulting patterns forming the creation are termed a vibrational pattern or energy pattern.

Each pattern is unique, for each is comprised of its own unique set of vibrations. Your vibrational pattern contains all of the vibrations that you have ever created. Therefore, you are actually a composite of the vibrations of all your creations melded together to form your unique energy or vibrational pattern.

ENERGY

Energy is the raw substance or material of creation that can be set in motion by a thought producing a vibration or creation that is either tangible or intangible. Energy is the latent possibilities of all existence, of all creation; all things that have been, are, or can be come from energy. Energy is the latent field of all-possibilities that when impacted by a thought forms a creation or vibrational pattern. Thoughts are like an electrical current flowing into the raw material of creation (energy that can form into any possibility) impacting or imprinting the energy forming a vibrational pattern from the latent possibilities within the energy.

Energy is the heart beat of what is and yet it is empty. Energy is empty, and yet it has all-possibilities latent within it ready to be placed into a creation or vibrational pattern of some type. You are energy, and you have energy. You can never run out of energy, for it shall always be. You cannot picture energy, grab hold of energy, or sense energy through the five physical senses in any definitive manner. Energy as it applies to your vibrational pattern is not tangible or a fixed hard substance. It is energy, the raw material of creation. Allow it to be a word that stands on its own.

Salem's definition of energy may be different from what you are accustom to, but do not let that throw you. In a scientific sense, energy is thought of in terms of how much work can be done, and certainly when we think of an energy crisis we are concerned with having a source of energy that can propel our cars, light our houses, or make things. We also think of energy in the sense of having a capacity of action or being a force of verbal expression. But Salem's use of the term is to describe the raw substance of creation in connection with the creation process, which is a much broader concept.

It is important to differentiate between energy and vibration. When you think you are feeling energy, you are really feeling the resulting vibration of the energy set into motion.

They are two different, distinct parts making up all creations including you. Energy is the raw substance of creation and vibration is the result of the energy set in motion by a thought.

There is a tendency, however, to use the word energy when from the definitions given, one might think vibration would be more accurate. For instance, vibrational patterns are also called energy patterns; chakras, which are vibrational patterns, are also termed energy centers. There is also a tendency to speak of a person's energy when actually the person's vibration would be a more fitting description. Because everything is energy vibrating or energy in motion, Salem commonly uses the word energy in connection with various terms and descriptions. The usage of energy in this manner, typically does not take away from what is meant but should not imply, in a very strict sense, that energy and vibration are equivalent.

Remember all things come from energy, and energy is simply the all-possibilities. You can think of energy as a mist or a tiny dynamic cell containing everything that has ever been or ever will be. But however you want to think of energy, it is as energy is activated that it takes its place among all other creations or what is termed a vibration. As energy becomes activated, it forms a vibration that manifests into a tangible or intangible part of your existence in your world.

CREATIONS / THOUGHT-FORMS

All thoughts create whether those thoughts show up in the physical or in other realms. In our daily lives, we think thoughts are just thoughts, but all thoughts produce creations affecting their environments having a life and a reality of their own. Once created, creations continue to exist even independent of the creator or person having the thought. Your creations will seek expression and manifestation whether materially or otherwise.

Your thoughts will actualize in the physical depending upon many circumstances corresponding to their configuration. They may appear as a very material, tangible item such as a new car or as non-tangible creations such as strained or happy relationships, anger, etc. You may not think of the non-tangible creations as creations, but they are just as numerous and have real effects. There is no doubt that an environment where anger is present is much different from the environment where joy is present.

For many, thoughts are not considered to have power so not much attention is paid to them. You therefore, do not correlate your thoughts with what manifests in your life. Your thoughts may manifest days or months or years later depending upon circumstances. Even the thoughts that are consistently reinforced and manifest readily may not be remembered or recognized. Your thoughts are so much apart of you that they seem invisible and you then wonder why certain things appear in your life. It really behooves you to pay attention to your thoughts.

Once your thoughts have created a creation two things happen: the creation will find its way to join other creations of like kind (like attracts like) strengthening the creation, and because the creation is your creation, it will always unite with your vibrational pattern. Is it any wonder why certain patterns seem to show up and repeat in your life?

When you create something, it is created forever. Creations exist forever because everything is in the now-moment.

You can never un-create one single thought you have had. Thoughts create, and those creations cannot return to nothingness, but you can transform and heal them. In chapter six, techniques will be given to help transform your creations through working with your chakra system.

As has been previously stated, all creations including you are simply a vibrational pattern that is energy set into motion. In the case of humanity, your vibrational pattern was initially set into motion by the Creator, and we shall leave it to you to define the Creator however you desire. (A discussion of the Creator is beyond the scope and purpose of this book, although Salem's views on the topic may be presented in another work at another time. The purpose here is to explore what the chakras are and how you can benefit from working with the chakra system in your life.)

Having defined the role of energy, thoughts and vibrational patterns as the basis for the creation of all things, let's look at this process with respect to the human soul or humanity.

The Components of the Vibrational Pattern

Your vibrational pattern can be broken down into various layers, bodies or components consisting of physical, mental, emotional and etheric bodies along with a system of chakras. These components are both tangible and intangible being vibrational patterns in their own right, for everything is energy in motion.

THE ETHERIC

Recognize that the creation of a human being, as you know it, had to be from a thought. (It is beyond the scope of this book to devise the trail that went from the original thought to what is known as humanity today.) As that original thought impacted energy, it formed a framework of what could be. That framework of possibilities is what Salem refers to as etheric energy or the etheric body.

The original thought creating the etheric body of a human being came from an all-possibility creator. Because that thought was so pure, the resulting etheric image contains all-possibilities. This is why it is said you are created in the image of your Creator. So the all-possibilities reside or are contained in the etheric body rather than in your fingers, internal organs, or even in your mind.

The etheric body is not solid in a physical sense, but it is out of this etheric body a physical human being is formed. The etheric is undefined, unemotional and not mental, being instead very light, pliable, and latent with all-possibilities. It is just the latent possibility of who you are, for the etheric body contains the possibilities of what you can create, change, become and do.

All things have etheric energy or vibrations because without etheric energies, you could not be a creative being. The etheric is the latent possibility, the image, and the framework from which all human creation began and those latent all-possibilities are still there. This is why you can grow, expand, and change things because you have the possibility to do that. This is why you have unlimited creative ability and are able to create whatever you choose whether it be chaos or harmony, a beautiful body or a body having limitations. There are always creative possibilities allowing you to create many things because the human etheric body contains all-possibilities.

Do not confuse energy with the etheric body. Energy is the vast void of untouched possibilities, the raw material of creation. An etheric body is energy having been imprinted upon and therefore is a vibrational pattern, a creation. An etheric body may not have taken a form other than energy, but the imprint is still there; it is no longer the raw, untouched, material of creation.

So what happens when you think a thought? When you think a thought, you imprint upon energy and create an etheric form. Now whether that creation manifests within the physical or not is another story, but all thoughts create.

From the etheric body a consciousness of thought formed creating a denser physical body. This is a part of the etheric expressing the human form. As the etheric began to form the physical, it was an outward expression of the latent possibilities within the etheric. That expression came from the etheric and is always a part of the etheric because it was a manifestation of expression within the etheric that shall always be.

Before a physical form can manifest, the etheric must set out the pattern for what then becomes the reflection in the physical. Thus, the etheric pattern will always be present first before the physical form manifests. For example, as a plant grows, the etheric pattern grows first and the physical follows. If you lose a portion of your body, it does not remove the pattern within the etheric. Only the reflection of the solid pattern in the physical is removed. The vibrational pattern was originally set in motion in the etheric, and now there is nothing that has evolved from that pattern. The etheric pattern still feels it has a job to do and will remain for some time attempting to reconstruct the physical. You may have heard how a person with an amputated limb may still feel the limb for a time after the amputation.

The etheric is the vibrational pattern in motion but not in a tangible form and even though it is not a third-dimensional pattern, it is a much stronger vibrational pattern.

THE CHAKRAS

As the physical formed from the etheric, and prior to the formation of the ego system and the belief in separation, there was a consciousness consisting of areas or centers to relate, guide, and define your existence of who you were and why you were. These centers of consciousness were created for the purpose of defining experience and allowing expression within the physical. As various attributes or aspects of consciousness were developed for defining experiences, distinct departments or energy centers formed. These centers would help define tangible aspects of experience such as this is grass, this water, this is blue, this is red, as well as being a means of expression for creativity, love, and will. Together these energy centers formed an interrelated system defining experiences in the physical. These energy centers are what we know and call today chakras.

Now, are your chakras in the etheric? Yes and no. These centers were created within the vibrational pattern and became part of the subtle anatomy being more etheric or energetic in nature but at the same time more aligned with the physical. This is difficult to describe, but if you think of de-

grees of fineness so-to-speak, like some sand is very coarse
and some sand is very fine, then the pure etheric is the finest
of sand and the physical is a coarse sand. The chakras are a
combination between the etheric and the physical; they interact having traits of the physical, and yet they do not have a
solid formation.

As mentioned in chapter two, when the ego system developed and experiences began to be analyzed within linear
time for the purpose of determining safety, the perceptions of
those experiences resulting from this process needed to be
stored for future use by the ego system. Being the unlimited
intelligence (even in limitation) you are, you adapted the
chakras to store the perceptions of your experiences. This most
likely came about because the chakras were already defining
and processing experiences (without limitation) within the
physical; therefore, it was natural for the perceptions of those
experiences to be stored also in the chakras. As you evolved
in the physical, the chakras began to function more as containers for storing the perceptions rather than centers for defining experience and allowing the flow of your expression
within the physical.

Today your vibrational pattern is filled with little energy
centers or perception containers (minor chakras) as the need
for further refinements in perceiving experience has evolved.
For instance, there is a perception container for beauty relat-
ing to how you perceive beauty, but you are not going to hear
of a beauty chakra. From this system of perception containers or chakras there are seven active major energy centers in
which the others ultimately feed into like tributaries of a river.
Together these energy centers primarily deal with your experience in the physical and your connection to the spiritual.

Again, to be true to the use of Salem's definitions, the chakras and the perceptions are simply vibrational patterns. You can think of the chakras as being a vibrational pattern of a container holding the vibrational patterns of the perceptions, but often the chakras are simply called energy centers.

THE AURA

If you can think of yourself simply as an energy pattern having a vibrational level or rate rather than thinking of yourself as a physical being, then you come to realize everything is merely energy in motion. A part of your point of consciousness that you think of as your human experience is in a physical pattern you can relate to, but a very large part is not in the physical but rather in the aura.

The aura is invisible and not something humanity can normally touch. Auras can be thought of as subtle, invisible or ethereal emanations having a distinctive but intangible quality surrounding a person or thing. Everything has an aura. Although auras are typically thought of as an energy field surrounding an object, the energy field also moves within the object or body as well.

The human aura is composed of a series of layers or subtle (intangible) bodies. These subtle bodies are also energy fields (vibrational patterns) containing thoughts, emotions, blockages, etc. The aura can be thought of as a composite energy field being made up of these subtle bodies. Each subtle body is a vibrational pattern consisting of things having similar characteristics pertaining to that body's particular nature.

The aura today primarily consists of a mental body and an emotional body surrounding the physical body. Your physi-

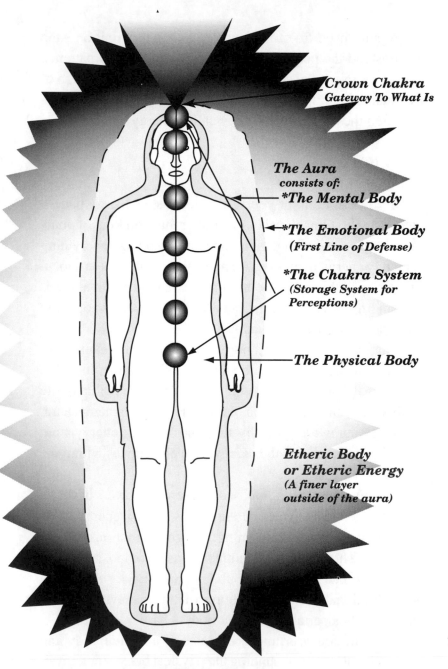

Crown Chakra
Gateway To What Is

The Aura
consists of:
*The Mental Body

*The Emotional Body
(First Line of Defense)

*The Chakra System
(Storage System for
Perceptions)

The Physical Body

**Etheric Body
or Etheric Energy**
(A finer layer
outside of the aura)

*Figure 2
Vibrational Pattern*

cal body being tangible and the other bodies are not. You may think of this as starting with a visible physical body surrounded by the energy of the mind called the mental body and outside of that is a layer where the emotions reside forming an outer layer of defense called the emotional body. All of that comprises your aura (see figure 2).

The human aura typically extends two to three feet outward from the body in all directions. Every part of your body and everything you experience in your life is contained somewhere in the aura. At times you may have sensed someone behind you even though you did not see, hear, or feel the person in a physical way. You knew someone was there because you felt his or her vibration brush up against your aura.

Again, when humanity began to live from experience rather than expression, the mental and emotional bodies began to be necessary. When it was deemed you had need for safety in an ego sense to protect youself, the mental and emotional bodies were formed around the physical body as an extension of the chakra system. The emotions are connected with the emotional body and your mental abilities of the mind (the analytical mind) with the mental body. The mental and emotional bodies are two main components making up the ego system.

Are the mental and emotional bodies in the etheric? The mental and emotional bodies do not have a solid form, so they are not physical in the sense that you can touch them and yet they are very much connected to physical experience. The mental and emotional bodies are more energetic, existing where energy interacts prior to physical interaction within the aura being more etheric in nature, but the aura is not the pure etheric. Going back to the sand example, the pure etheric is beyond the aura in degrees of fineness. The etheric is a layer above the aura being the beautiful framework where this creative process takes place. In contrast, the emotional and mental bodies are not latent with all-possibilities; they are merely storage containers of information that trigger based on your perspective of whether you are safe or not.

Think of the aura as energy that emanates from you, which is the emotional and mental body as an extension of the chakras. The aura is a result of what radiates out from your soul's physical experience. Thus when you see an aura, you are primarily seeing what is emanating from a person's physical state of consciousness as it affects their mental and emotional bodies. As a consequence, auras vibrate and change with your physical, emotional, mental, and spiritual states.

When people today see auras or take pictures of auras, they often see colors. Those colors are chakra colors expressing within the aura. If you did not have an emotional or mental body, you would still have an aura, but the aura would be more like a halo, a light, or a light body, not necessarily an aura with different colors in it. Without the mental and emotional bodies, the aura would just be a brilliant, gold light. But remember, the chakras began to store perceptions, and the mental and emotional bodies were created as an extension of the chakras (all part of the ego system) when safety became a concern. If you no longer had the need for a mental and an emotional body, you would no longer be living from perceptions of experiences. Thus what would be emanating from the physical consciousness into the aura would be totally different.

THE EMOTIONAL BODY

The emotional body is the body furthest out in the energy field of your aura and is the first line of defense for the ego system. Everything entering your energy field must first come through the emotional body. You may think all of your experiences are analyzed by the mind first and then your emotions are activated. Sometimes the mind does indeed trigger the emotional field, but the mental body is inside of the emotional body and, therefore, all things pass through the emotions before reaching the mental body. Every experience will, therefore, go through the emotional body before either the chakra system or the mental or physical bodies are affected. Because the emotional body is so much more energetic, it picks up the vibrations or happenings within the experiences actually quicker than the chakra system.

Watch how you feel about things and determine for yourself, for instance, whether the mind is always first to be engaged and whether permission is given before, say, the emotion of anger wells up. Or is it before you know it anger has taken control, and you are mentally trying to figure out how to calm down the energy of the situation your emotions have stirred up. Pay attention and decide for yourself. The results may be interesting.

Created as your first line of defense, the emotions are contained in the energy field of the emotional body residing in the outer most part of the aura and together with the chakra system greatly affects how you respond to your experiences.

THE MENTAL BODY

When you had a need to remember your experiences linearly within time, the mental body was created. Now, of course, you could always think, but the conscious mind did not have the capacity at this stage in the evolution of human existence to remember your experiences, let alone from all of your lifetimes. The mental body, therefore, was created to store every thought you have ever had as a soul expressing and experiencing in the third-dimension, physical, universe.

The mental body analyzes your experiences by what your past experiences have been and how those experiences related to your safety. Thus, your mental body plays a powerful part in how you relate to the experiences in your life and is a key component of the ego system located within the aura.

The chakras, the emotional and mental bodies essentially act as one; they are not really separate. The mental and emotional bodies are an extension or a part of what you do: they are a part of how you create and how you experience. The mental and emotional bodies store data and react to your experiences from your particular view of safety. Because the interaction between these bodies and the chakras is so instantaneous, it is difficult for the conscious mind to distinguish what happens first within the system. For example, a truck comes towards you and you jump, or here comes an old friend you have not seen for many years, and you feel good. The experience first hits the emotional body and then is processed accordingly within the vibrational pattern. Information is constantly being transferred back and forth, to and from, these bodies and the chakras. It all happens very quickly. The chakras, the mental body, and the emotional body are all interconnected and work together as a unit.

Your chakras have come to form a system of holding perceptions that limit you, and all creations in that expression emanate from the etheric body. The intricacies and workings of this system are very complex. You can find within the various chakra literatures, other layers described or definitions given that may differ from the manner in which Salem describes the attributes of the aura. These differences may have more to do with points of view and preferences of terminology in describing a complex system and should be taken by the reader relative to the descriptions found in this book or in other literature.

The main aim of Salem's message is to evolve the ego by helping you to remember who you are and to become self-aware. The finer details and points of view of your creative existence will be uncovered and discovered however you choose. For the purpose of exploring the chakra system from the Salem point of view, the primary focus shall be with the physical, emotional, and mental bodies of the vibrational pattern.

Summary

The human etheric body came from thought latent with all-possibilities. From those possibilities within the etheric body, you created and manifested from the outward projection of your thoughts and desires. As you did, these creations were all in the etheric, and you initially related only on an etheric level. Then by choice these projections, or creations became denser, having a beauty unique to the physical form. Truly there is a beauty to the solid, third-dimensional form that is not in the etheric. All of this has been a long journey.

As the physical formed, centers of consciousness were associated with the human physical form that today are known as your chakras. As these centers of consciousness or chakras became more aligned with the physical and the separation, it was not long before you were living from experience rather than expression. The moment you began to live from experience was the moment the mental and emotional bodies became necessary and were formed or created from the etheric, for the etheric contains the latent creative possibilities from which all creations must originate.

The chakras and their extension, the emotional and mental bodies, are where all of your experiences and expressions, including past lives, can be energetically placed within the aura. There is no separation between the etheric, the physical, the mental, or emotional bodies; they are all intertwined. In an attempt to explain how things work for the mind, they are discussed separately, but they are one because they are all part of the original creation expressing—the etheric expressing. Hence think of it as one.

Chakras are the means through which you express, but they also have become the containers holding the perceptions of your experiences. Without storing the perceptions of the experiences, the chakras are aspects of consciousness defining physical experience in an unlimited manner while bringing a richness and fullness of expressing life.

Everything that becomes stored in the aura and expressed from the etheric has a great affect upon you. The consciousness of your mental body greatly influences how your mind thinks, and the emotional body determines your response to events and the people in your life. Every thought you have is not only stored in the physical cells of your body but also in your chakra system as well as the mental and emotional bodies of your aura. This is a powerful creation, which you do not always realize and give it the credit it deserves.

In order to move back into the spiritual power of who you are, the ego system must evolve and your limitations healed. You cannot be in your power if you are letting your emotional body dictate how you are experiencing the planet. You must return to your power recognizing the emotions are there but not allowing them to be the dictator of your life.

Perhaps this will be clearer if viewed from another perspective. If mentally you just keep holding on to something, whatever it might be, the healing process can be very slow. If emotionally you are set into a pattern of fear, then the emotions become very strongly tied to the fear pattern whatever it may be. These things appear in the physical body in some manner, for the physical is just the outward reflection of what is inside. You then notice your body is impaired in some way and try to remedy the body, but all healing must start in these layers or bodies within the aura. Physcial healing cannot fully take place until mental and emotional healing has occurred. Now that may just be a sliver in those bodies, but it is impossible for the physical to heal completely until those slivers have healed.

The message is simple: this is what you are dealing with but come back and stand in your power. To this end, the chakra system plays a large role in healing and evolving the ego system. Through understanding and working with the chakra system, you will discover a fundamental tool you can use to help remove limitation and evolve the ego as you progress on your spiritual journey.

5

****

HOW THE CHAKRA SYSTEM
AFFECTS YOUR LIFE

Within your vibrational pattern the bodies serve one function and the chakras serve another. The chakras are connected to each other and to the other parts of your vibrational pattern: the physical body, emotional body, and mental body. Therefore, the chakra system does not stand alone nor is it isolated within the vibrational pattern.

Every thought you have is stored somewhere in your vibrational pattern whether in the emotional, mental, or physical body. Every time you have a thought, it alters you. Each thought alters the vibrational pattern you have created as your soul journeys on the planet at this moment. All of those idle thoughts you do not stop to consider or are unaware of, are continually changing you!

Just as the emotional and mental bodies are not normally seen, even though there is no doubt emotions and mental activity are parts of everyone's life, so, too, the chakra system is not normally seen but continually affects your life. Every thought, experience, and action you have feed somewhere into this system of chakras. Everything you touch, see, sense, or feel flows into and are stored within these seven energy centers. No matter what else is in your vibrational pattern, everything flows in or out of these energy centers and is affected by the seven major chakras.

As the perceptions of an experience are processed by the chakra system, the energy of the perceptions is split into parts and stored within the various chakras. Therefore, you may have an experience affecting all of the chakras or just one or two, but in every moment of your life, you are filtering the perceptions of your experiences into these containers.

Your mental and emotional bodies are very connected and together they determine how you will experience your next experience through analysis of the information coming from the chakras. The bodies use the perceptions stored within the chakras as a source of information for analysis in the mental body and as a source for triggering the emotions in the emotional body. In their current state, the chakras serve as a reservoir of limiting information used by the other portions of your vibrational pattern to determine your safety and consequently, how you respond and choose your experiences. Therefore, the chakras do not directly determine your next experience as much as they *block* your expression.

This is why clearing the perceptions from the chakras is so beneficial. When the other bodies within your vibrational pattern seek information from the chakras upon which to base their analysis upon, there is no information from the perceptions of experiences to cause the analysis to limit you. By clearing these blockages within the chakras, you will interpret things differently because the message held within the chakras will be different. Clearing the chakras, therefore, literally changes the vibration of your vibrational pattern.

Fear and the Chakras

In the beginning the chakras did not contain fear, for you did not know fear. The chakras processed and defined experience without fear. As the analytical mind became more predominant, it began to analyze the experiences from the perception of your separateness from the Creator, and fear began to be a part of your experiences.

Fear is defined as any emotion, for that is what fear is. You created emotions as a defense mechanism when you perceived you had a need to ensure your safety. As your experiences produced emotions, the emotions began to create pockets of fear, tiny blemishes, within the chakras. The fear (blemishes) began to limit and distort your creative power. As you became limited by the fear, you began to analyze and determine your tomorrows based upon your yesterdays to determine how you could best function and navigate in this third-dimensional world you created. It all began with the collection of perceptions in the energy centers or the chakras.

If, on one hand, within a short period of time you have several painful experiences of the same nature, the vibrations of the perceptions become strengthened and you can become out of balance in this particular area. You have allowed your vibration to become focused on a narrow part of your experience dictated by the perceptions of past experiences. Your perceptions, therefore, have become so entrenched within your chakras they distort your clarity and balance of what you experience.

If, on the other hand, you have a period in which you think you are blessed with good luck, three or four fortunate things happen to you one right after the other, then life could not be better. Those vibrations likewise are strengthened and continue to draw more of the same to you. Consequently, your view of your world is constantly being colored in one direction or the other based upon past perceptions causing the view of your current experience to be distorted.

Recognize what is happening in an experience is not just a thinking process. You can only hold a controlled thought for a limited period of time, but your perceptions work day and night in every area of your being: within your mind, physical body, and emotional body. Your vibration is continually controlled by perception.

You are the creator of your world, and you have the capability of creating whatever you desire. Unfortunately, the fear vibrations you have collected in your chakras distort your desires. At this stage in your evolution in the physical, it is difficult to imagine just how limiting this is to you and how much freedom you can have as you clear these vibrations.

How the Chakras Affect Your Decisions

There are many hidden components affecting your decision-making process. What you think of as your conscious mind accounts for only a small percentage of this process. This is because your decisions are first processed through the mass consciousness, all of the societal controls you have chosen to live within, your chakra system which is going to process the results of all of your experiences, your subconscious mind, and finally the conscious mind is allowed a role in the process.

The subconscious is connected to the chakras and draws from the perceptions of every experience you have ever had within the physical. Many times, before the analytical mind has ever had a chance to look at a situation, the subconscious has already decided how to approach the situation based on information the conscious mind no longer remembers. Now you are not very aware of your subconscious mind unless you are able to hold a meditative or hypnotic state aligned with the subconscious mind, therefore you may not be aware of the significant role the subconscious plays in your daily life.

Through the subconscious and the analytical mind, your consciousness is connected vibrationally to every thought that has ever been or will be. The mental, vibrational consciousness has no boundaries and neither do the emotions. Your connection to these thoughts plays a large role in determining how you choose to experience your world though you may not be consciously aware of it. It is a very elaborate system of guidance. There are levels (or filters) determining how much credence and importance your particular consciousness gives to those thoughts and how you choose to arrange them in your belief system.

By the time you consciously make a decision, you have eliminated millions of possibilities. Your chakra system eliminates many of the possibilities, and your subconscious filters even more. By the time your conscious mind actively participates, much has been automatically determined. It all stems from your past-life experiences connected to the lower three chakras feeding into the subconscious which has the ability to analyze from the perceptions stored within the chakras. Of course, you have the opportunity to gather new perceptions and to either alter, transform, or build upon them, and you do this constantly. This is your life process, but your decisions, which affect your existence, are arrived at through a much larger process than just the conscious mind alone, and the chakra system plays a key role in this process.

The Chakras and Success in Life

If you are experiencing less than what you desire to be perfect in your life, then recognize you may be *perceiving* at some level of consciousness that the attainment of what you desire would create pain. As you set goals and work to attain what you think would make the perfect life situation, realize you filter through a tremendous amount of unknown perceptions. If any of those perceptions conclude that pain will result from the attainment of your goal or perfect life situation, then you may block the creation of what you desire in your life.

For instance, if two lifetimes ago you had what you perceived to be the perfect relationship and this relationship caused some type of a painful experience, then while you are not consciously aware of that experience in this lifetime, you may never-the-less not allow the creation or attainment of the perfect relationship. This is a blockage to what you perceive to be success.

Blockage shall be defined as an obstacle that must be overcome in order to reach your desired goal or life experience. The very function of the blockage is to stop what will create more pain. Recognize all of the perceptions stored in your chakras can impede or block the creation of what you desire. Therefore, in order to open the possibilities in your life and attain the success you desire, clearing or transforming the perceptions within the chakras can be a key prerequisite. This is especially true if you are consciously unaware of the experiences forming the perceptions blocking your success.

The Chakras and Your Everyday Life

When you are so wrapped up with the concerns of the ego (judgments, deadlines, perceived important issues) that your energy or vibration becomes knotted, you take yourself out of the flow with Spirit and weigh yourself down. You can become argumentative, have less patience, and begin to view things as wrong (judge). These are the signs you are weighed down with the ego and need to transform the limitations of your creations of judgment through the perceptions of worry, fear, and doubt. Transforming your limitations will allow you to live from Spirit and flow.

Living from Spirit is living in peace, joy, harmony, and Love. One way to lighten the heavy vibration of the ego's concerns is through clearing your chakras. This process transforms the perceptions and blockages within the chakras, making your energy lighter (raising your vibration) and thereby easier to live from Spirit. The more you align with Spirit the less you will judge, and the more you will be in harmony with everything around you. You will not take what people say as personal. You are following you, and you are safe within that knowledge.

Now is the time to increase your awareness and understanding of how going beyond your physical senses can affect your life. It is important to understand the integral part the chakras or energy centers play in your daily life:

> ➢ How your perceptions of experiences have limited you to the point of being unable to express as the unlimited, powerful spiritual being that you are.
> ➢ How the blockages within the chakras hold you in limitation, and how easy it is to clear these blockages, thereby, empowering your entire vibrational pattern.

The way for you to remove your limitation is to clear the blockages stored in the chakras caused by the perceptions and fears from this lifetime and past lifetimes. The lower three chakras, in particular, are truly compacted with perceptions, fears, blockages, and limitations of your experiences within the physical.

6

****

WORKING WITH THE CHAKRA SYSTEM

How can you tune in and become aware of your inner source sustaining your existence, so you can move into the power that you are? How can you do that when your vibrational pattern is restricted by the perceptions of all of your experiences within the physical?

It can be a difficult task if you are unaware of the obstacles in your way. You read, you think, and work very hard attempting to move into your Divinity. But the path to Divinity is not through the understanding of your analytical mind rather it is a matter of listening to yourself, trusting in yourself, and knowing you are safe as you begin to change your vibrational field. Clearing the chakras is an important step in being able to center yourself in the power that you are. This will aid you in recognizing your unlimited being-ness and the possibilities of your creative existence.

Your vibrational pattern and the chakra system are far more complex than can be described in words. To express these technicalities and describe the great complexity of this system is only for the analytical mind. Recognize the chakra system is not something easily translated into language and information you are able to totally comprehend. But the analytical mind typically needs some minimal understanding in order to be willing to move forward with the process that will bring your creative vibrational fields into alignment.

Recognize What Is Taking Place

Everything, all possibilities are yours. That is a given. You have unlimited, creative power, but your belief system is based upon past perceptions of experiences you know nothing about. Recognize how you are living your life from the confusion of perceptions that are dominating and creating strong vibrations, which in turn attract more of the same to you. You then wonder why you are repeatedly experiencing these things in your life.

How can this be changed? Perceptions are the individualized response or reaction to your life process. You, therefore, need to understand how your perceptions limit your life and the steps you can take to free yourself from these limitations.

Begin to clear this confusion by understanding how the chakras affect your life, clearing the chakras, and choosing to take the action of living your experiences fully every day. There is no way you can begin to live in expression until you clear the perceptions from the chakras. Perceptions are blockages within your vibrational pattern preventing your expression. When you give yourself *permission* to release these blockages and allow them to be transformed, the chakras begin to have the richness and the fullness they first had when you began to create and put energy into a form.

Clear your chakras. Remove the blockages so you are not feeling afraid and limited. Daily take time to clear your chakras. Know it is safe to clear the chakras.

Do not think of who you are as tied to your chakras. Clearing the chakras is a necessary step to know who you are, and this does not make the chakras bad. Chakras are needed for the flow of energy within your creative process, but to manifest your desires easily also requires the chakras to be free of fear and limitation.

Only The Perceptions Need To Be Cleared

Your chakra system, mental body, emotional body, physical body, and subconscious already have a memory of your experiences. Your response to these experiences has formed your perceptions, but it does not matter how the chakras came to their current vibrational states.

It is what the chakras contain and how your perceptions are creating blockages affecting your vibrational pattern that is important.

The beautiful part to freeing your vibrational pattern of the blockages and limitations is that only the perceptions are required to be cleared. You do not have to know what the experiences are nor remember and analyze the experiences causing the limitations or blockages. You only need to clear the confusion of the perception. Experiences are neither right nor wrong, good nor bad; they are just experiences, but it is important to be willing to let go of your perception of those experiences.

Remember, everything is simply a vibrational pattern emanating vibrations, and what you really relate to is vibration. The chakras are the vibrational centers that contain the vibrations of the perceptions of all of your experiences. It is your perception of the experience that determines what kind of vibration is created and stored within the chakra system. When you clear the chakras, it is not the experiences you are clearing but rather the perceptions of those experiences causing the vibrations to be blocked. You are not removing the experiences, for that is why you chose to be physical to begin with: to experience the physical, to express in a third-dimensional form. You are only limiting yourself by the perceptions of those experiences.

You may think there are some perceptions that are pretty good, and therefore may not be willing to let go of those perceptions. But the more you are willing to let go and clear all of your perceptions, the more Divinity floods into the chakras, and what you thought was the most something could be, explodes into a great expansion for you.

Going Beyond the Mind

Every thought, experience, and action you have feeds into the chakra system as a stored perception. You may think, "I will just change my mind about the experience". But the perceptions are not in your mind. Perceptions are buried in your chakra system having a unique vibration and life force designed to protect you, but also limit you.

The chakra system is a self-automated, autonomous system you long ago put in place for your own protection because you could not and still cannot consciously think of all of the experiences you perceive to affect your safety. Lifetime after lifetime you bring these stored perceptions back into your vibrational pattern. You could spend your entire life attempting to mentally figure out the perceptions formed from each of these thoughts, experiences, and actions and still be unable to remember and clear them all. It would take lifetimes to go through all of the perceptions that have accumulated, and the process would only build more perceptions!

Now the mind loves being part of the action. The mind likes to know what the experiences and the perceptions are so it can take action. But the mind does not have the ability to track all of your perceptions or to clear them because the mind is filled with its own concept of fear, pain, limitation and the danger they present to your existence. The process may be fun and interesting, and the mind may have a great time doing it, but the result of trying to clear the perceptions in this manner will be weak and short in duration. Consequently, there is no way you are going to clear all of the perceptions within the chakras by mental, emotional or physical work. A different means is required to clear the perceptions from the chakras.

The Seven Energy Pathways

There are different means to work with energy or vibrational patterns, and the methods described in this book is certainly not the only way. People have made attempts to work with their chakra systems, to balance and harmonize the system, and undoubtedly positive effects are felt. But at times, these attempts only result in the vibrations being rearranged with large amounts of blocked energy (vibrations) still needing to be cleared.

To help you more effectively clear your chakras, seven Energy Pathways have been anchored on the planet and are available for your use. These pathways are simply a gift to the world from those in the universe who love you.

What are Energy Pathways, and why do you need them? Remember everything is energy in motion or vibrational patterns. Vibrational patterns can bump against other vibrational patterns, co-mingle, etc. All is one, so you are connected to all of the emotions and the distortions of the mass consciousness. You are a part of it because you are a soul experiencing and expressing in the humanity of mass consciousness. When you set intent, the intent may have to navigate through these vibrational patterns becoming distorted. The Energy Pathways are clear, vibrational fields without interference or resistance, so your intent to transform the vibrations within your chakras will not become distorted, and the clearing process is more effective.

The Energy Pathways have cut a path for you through the vibrations of the mass consciousness and are maintained in the same manner as your roads are maintained. You are not required to do anything to maintain these pathways. They are maintained and kept open for you, but just as a road you may choose to use the Energy Pathways or not. The Energy Pathways are available any time you choose to use them.

You may see these pathways as light or as anything that helps you to accept and utilize these pathways. Remember, the pathways are clear vibrational paths without distortion.

Your intent to enter the Energy Pathways simply puts you there.

Clearing the perceptions from the chakras is, therefore, not difficult. You have unlimited power and can do anything, but at times it can be difficult to go beyond the ego system and the mass consciousness. The Energy Pathways were established to be a powerful tool to help you go beyond the mass consciousness. You are encouraged to use them, but it is your choice. To clear the chakras without the Energy Pathways is like trudging over rocky terrain with a horse and buggy versus a jet. You can do it, and you can get there, but it is so much easier using the pathways!

Clearing the Chakras

Until you clear the vibrations of your perceptions from the chakras, you are asking a monumental task of yourself to be the spiritual being you know resides within you and creates without limitation. There are a few steps you can use daily to remove the effects of the perceptions stored in your chakras. It is not difficult to clear these vibrations, but it is a choice you must make.

STEPS FOR CLEARING THE CHAKRAS

Step 1 – Center yourself, quieting your thoughts and with your intent connect the seven Energy Pathways to your seven major chakras.

Step 2 – With your intent, allow all of the blocked vibrations and limiting perceptions stored within your chakra system to enter the Energy Pathways.

Step 3 – Send these blocked vibrations and limiting perceptions through the Energy Pathways and into the Universal Consciousness of Love or pure, Divine Love allowing Love to heal and transform them. If you prefer, you can send these blocked vibrations and perceptions into a golden, white light where they are wrapped in the Divine Love of God or the universe, whatever Divine Love means to your mind.

Step 4 – Finally, allow all of these healed and transformed vibrations to return to you through the Energy Pathways and back to the originating chakras where they then heal, free, and empower you.

These four steps are suggested for clearing your chakras. You can use any other visuals or means you are comfortable with to clear these vibrations. But the key elements should entail: setting your *intent* to clear the chakras and release the blockages, allowing Love to heal and transform the blocked vibrations and limiting perceptions, and having the resulting healed and transformed vibrations being returned to you to empower your vibrational pattern. The reasons for the four steps are as follows:

> ➢ Centering yourself and quieting your thoughts will enhance your focus and ability to clearly set your intent.
> ➢ Setting *intent* is the activator for your will and thus a key part of the process. You can tune into the chakras and sense how clogged they are but that does not matter. The key is to set your intent to clear the blockages.
> ➢ Allowing the blocked vibrations and perceptions to be wrapped in Love heals and transforms them removing the limitation and thus is another major step.
> ➢ Having the healed and transformed vibrations being returned to you, allows you to be empowered from the process.

It is suggested you use the Energy Pathways to help clear these blockages easily and not with a lot of work, but that is your choice. The Energy Pathways are clear vibrational fields of intent anchored because everything is energy—energy in motion. You connect the pathways to each of your chakras and release the blockages and limiting perceptions stored in your chakras simply with your intent.

Do not have thoughts or lingering doubts you might clear something you need. This will not happen. All you are doing is allowing anything within your vibrational pattern that limits you to be cleared. Remember, once you create something, it is created forever. Once you have a thought it is yours for eternity, therefore you are not going to get rid of any creation. You may want to deny them, or not claim them, but they are your creations and a part of you. Your creations are your responsibility, but you can transform and heal those creations limiting you.

Therefore, send your blockages and limiting perceptions into the Universal Consciousness of Love, Divine Love, God, or whatever feels comfortable to you, for unconditional love can heal all things. You see, there is only fear and Love and Love is the reality. Fear is the ego belief system (the illusion) that creates all limitations. Love is the vibration emanating from the Creator as the first vibration coming through energy. As such Love is the highest vibration capable of interacting with every vibration that exists. That is why Love is unlimited, total, complete and all encompassing. Love knows no limitations and has no limitations. Love cannot be diluted or affected by any vibrations other than its own. Therefore, Love is the great healer, and when you send your blockages into the field of Love, it heals and transforms the fear and now the vibrations that limited you returns to empower you.

Finally, you must trust. You must trust not in some outside force but in yourself. You must trust you have an unlimited Spirit, the God essence of creation manifested in your soul, which is your individualized expression of your creative power desiring to come forth. You are only Love, and Love desires to express through you; it is only the perceptions that limit you.

Clear the chakras everyday for thirty days, and in the days to follow you will begin to feel different. You will begin to experience life in ways not conceived of today. You will enjoy life more, and at the end of thirty days you will be well on your way to transforming the blockages and limitations affecting your life. Now typically, you will not clear it all in thirty days, but if you are at least consistent for that length of time, you will begin to see within yourself the truth of what is being said.

Clearing the chakras is an important step you can take to open the possibilities in your life. Be assured what you are doing will have a great effect and benefit in the days and months to come. Subtle changes will be seen in how you react to the events, circumstances, and people you encounter in your life. You will open spiritually, and your vibrational pattern will change.

Clearing the chakras is similar to moving mounds and mounds of dirt or in this case blockages so a solid foundation can be laid for the new. You may feel these vibrations move or you may not. If you do, it simply means you are sensitive to these vibrations. If you do not, it only means you are not tuned into this vibrational level, but it does not mean it is not happening!

The more you allow yourself to become comfortable connecting to the Energy Pathways, and giving yourself permission to clear the chakras, it then becomes a simple and quick process of allowing the clearing to take place. Blockages taking years to clear before can now be cleared in days due to the Energy Pathways.

Methods described in this book are not meant to compete with any other methods you may be using to work with the chakras. The method described is one suggested method for clearing the chakras and it does not matter which method is proclaimed right, wrong, or best; but rather what works for you. What is important is to clear the blockages limiting your life's possibilities.

Effects of the Clearing Process

SAFETY NET OF FEAR

It is important that you are comfortable and feel safe with the process of clearing your chakras. In the beginning you may find yourself uncomfortable with the process. You may find yourself a bit lost in what you are feeling, sensing, or doing because you are going beyond the safety net created by the ego system. Therefore, you may want to run back to what is familiar and feels safe. Realize you have lived within the parameters of fear for so long fear is what you know. It is clearly part of the ego system. It is like being given a clear shot at something, but you have no instructions of what to do with it. That is when it is important to connect to your inner Divinity and become aware of the spiritual essence within you. This is where the upper chakras come into play.

Recognize your ego system will attempt to keep you safe in the only way it knows how as you take the steps to clear your chakra system of the fears you hold. This can sometimes reach an uncomfortable level, but if you recognize this is only the existence of your fears and continue to allow the choice of healing, you will move beyond the fear to the place you desire to be. There is no way to tell you where you are going, for your mind does not have the data to analyze it and therefore has difficulty understanding it.

Shifts will occur in your daily living, in your perceptions, and how you react to the events and situations in your life. As this happens, life will begin to take on a different reality and this is how you will recognize the truth of what is being said. As you clear your fears and allow the Love to flow, your life will be better, so be aware of what is taking place, and allow yourself to integrate the shifts.

The ego system has protected you lifetime after lifetime through its own checks and balances. As you begin to remove these checks and balances, you may begin to feel as though there is nothing to hold on to, but as you continue, you will move into a greater expansiveness of who you are, into a place of peace, power, joy, Love and harmony. The things you now struggle with so desperately will begin to flow for you.

PAST MEMORIES

As you allow yourself to become free of your perceptions, the clearing may trigger the memory of some of your past experiences. Just realize this is a past experience being triggered within the mental body. Your mental body stores every experience you ever had, so if the memory of some experience is triggered, recognize what it is, and *detach* from the experience.

You will find it is beneficial to detach as you work with the chakra system. Your experience need not be replayed so that it is again felt in the emotional chakra, for then instead of clearing the perception you only further compact the vibrations within the chakras.

Most of the time memories are not triggered, but if it happens, recognize it is a past experience, and you are perfectly safe. Detach from the experience, and let the Energy Pathways clear those perceptions from your chakra system.

CHAKRA CLEARING & HEALING

Chakra clearing and healing go hand in hand. Often healing is thought of in terms of physical wounds, but what is being referred to are the wounds resulting from the pain and fear festering from within. Within are the pain, fear, and limitation resulting from the subjective observance of your experiences forming perceptions. This can be reflected in your body as an illness or in an intangible form such as troubled relationships or emotional wounds. The experience cannot be changed, for that is your existence, but the perceptions can be transformed. Ultimately all healing is about perceptions and is why clearing the chakras is beneficial to the healing process.

When the chakras are clear, the healing process is more effective. Healing with clogged chakras is like trying to heal a wound that has not been cleaned. Clear chakras allow a nice clean heal of the wound, so as you clear the chakras, you will experience more healing.

You think of healing as feeling better, but healing is really a process of realigning and recognizing. It does not need to be painful. It is only as you resist the process of realignment and recognition of your truth, your expression, and your awareness that the wounds are reopened and that can be painful.

Chakra Clearing – An Ongoing Process

As the days go by, you will see the effects of clearing the chakras, but the results will not be instantaneous. You will feel differently about things, but of course you are still living daily life on the planet. The chakras are neither static nor stagnant. You are continually processing and feeding energy into the chakras based upon your experiences. Be aware of what you are placing back into your chakras by your words, thoughts, actions, and feelings. The Energy Pathways do much of the work for you in clearing the chakras, but they cannot stop what you are placing back into the chakras. The total transformation has not yet become a reality, so clearing the chakras should not be considered a one-time event, but an ongoing and continuing process.

As you clear your chakras, recognize what you are experiencing, how some of the fears have healed, what you feel, and when you are not feeling safe. If you are feeling unsafe about your finances, home, relationships, career, etc., recognize you still have fears latent within the ego system, If a little fear raises its head, do not try to determine if this is a fear from some relationship six lifetimes ago. It does not matter. Do not try to define whether the fear is in your emotional, survival, or heart chakra because it can be in all of them. Simply with your *intent* connect the Energy Pathways to your chakras, taking a moment to allow Love to clear these fears. Love will heal the emotion you are feeling in all of the chakra areas, and you will begin to feel a shift no longer feeling so unsafe. It is really a great time to live on the planet. You can manifest whatever you desire.

The words safe or unsafe are used instead of the word

afraid because that is what it is all about. When you feel safe, you do not feel fear.

YOU ARE THE EXPERT OF YOUR JOURNEY

The expression of your desires can be manifested in many different ways. For instance, you may desire chocolate and the universe gives it to you in the form of candy, cake, pie, or cookies. Sometimes you will not experience chocolate the same as someone else does, but the expression will be the same. When you are feeling peace for instance, it may come to you in different formulas as needed to help you align your experiences and heal your latent fears, but there will still be peace.

If what you experience is different from somebody else's experience, do not allow their experience to be deemed the "right" experience. There are no experts on the planet. Even the most advanced souls have not become the experts. You are the expert of your journey; take charge of it, and design your journey the way you desire it to be.

ASK FOR HELP

Remember to ask for help. There is much help for you in the universe. Ask the angels, the ascended masters, or your spirit guides, etc. They are all anxious and willing to be of service but cannot and will not interfere with your free will. Therefore, you must ask, for they can do nothing unless you ask, and you do forget to ask. Call upon them and they will be there to help you.

The Results Of Clearing Your Chakras

If you spend the time to connect the Energy Pathways and clear your chakras regularly, there will be great rewards for you. You will feel the difference, your life will reflect the difference, and you will begin to glimpse and understand your expansiveness. As you lessen the affect of your perceptions, you will express more freely and in totality becoming more aware and able to move into and express from your awareness.

Your vibrational pattern sends out a vibration and creates the reflection of who you think you are in the physical body. As the vibrational pattern begins to be healed and transformed, your vibration will change. You will vibrate at a higher level. This may result in changes, for instance, in your sleeping patterns or eating habits. As you clear the base chakra, you may have different tastes for food. As you clear your emotional chakra, you may be more sensitive to vibrations. You may find your appearance changes; you are more radiant, more at peace, and more connected to life as fear is removed from your vibrational pattern.

BEING OUT OF STEP WITH OTHERS

As you remove the blockages and clear the confusion, you will not perceive in the same way, and therefore may be out of step with those around you. Remember, others may still be living from the confusion and may think you have absolutely lost all of your sense of reality. Allow them to live where they choose, but that does not have to be your choice, for you are now the expert of your journey!

You will be greatly rewarded as you honor and allow yourself to focus on the source of your creativity, your vibrational pattern, and your chakra system. At this time, you probably do not realize how important this is, but in the days and months ahead you will see the effects, for this will empower all you do in your life.

You cannot heal and transform these vibrations without feeling the effects of these cleared vibrations as they come back to you. For you see, you are going to be a different vibrational pattern from the pattern you are today. You will be more comfortable with who you are, having more inner peace, more balance, more harmony, and your creations will manifest faster. More importantly, your creations will be undistorted.

The chakras are a basic part of your vibrational pattern and the information on the chakras is like the ABCs of who you are. Once you have learned the ABCs and recognize how to use them, then they become useful to you. You can then begin to put things together within your vibrational pattern to create what you desire. It is a fascinating journey as you begin to understand yourself in ways that perhaps you never have before.

Remember, no one can do it for you. It is your journey, your responsibility, and your delight to live in this beautiful, physical plane. Enjoy your journey. Have fun with it and allow physical existence to be the playground it was intended to be. Clear those perceptions. It is well worth the time you spend every day to clear the chakras.

In the remainder of this book, the sphere of influence of each of the seven active major chakras, along with the potentials and areas of limitation will be explored.

Part II

The Seven Major Chakras

The chakras play an integral part in your existence and daily life on the planet. Understanding and working with the chakras is an important step in being able to center yourself in the power that you are, recognizing your unlimited being-ness and the possibilities of your creative existence.

7

****

THE SURVIVAL CHAKRA

As your ego system developed, you adapted the chakras to hold the vibrations of your experiences. This was necessary so there could be a continuity of experience within linear time, but the chakras were never intended to hold limitation. As you began to fear your existence within the physical, the chakras began to clog, and the first place this became evident was in your base or survival chakra.

The base or survival chakra is located at the base of the spine and contains every vibration that has ever threatened your survival on the planet during any lifetime. If you ever felt physical existence was not safe for you to exist, then all of the perceptions of those experiences over all of your lifetimes are stored in the survival or base chakra. Every experience that has ever threatened your physical existence or harmed you in any way, whether that was just stubbing your toe, having a tragic accident, or someone taking your life, the perception of fear of those experiences are stored in the survival chakra. At times you are afraid of being physical and wish to escape physical, but you are also afraid of not being physical as well. As long as you fear for your existence in any way, the survival chakra is restricted.

You may fear loving or being loved. You may fear your sexuality or have a difficult time expressing what is within your soul, but your survival is what you fear the most. This is a tremendous amount of vibrations causing your base or survival chakra to be the heaviest chakra having the most vibrations stored within it. Therefore, the survival chakra is one of the most compacted energy centers within the chakra system and, consequently, controls much of your choice of experience.

Survival instincts are also stored within the base/survival chakra. Survival instincts determine what you must do to stay on the planet rather than to be safe on the planet. Survival instincts include: I must eat food, I must drink water, and I must sleep. These are things you believe you must do to survive. Recognize these instincts are your creations. Be aware as you clear the survival chakra, your instincts may well arise and give you an opportunity to recognize them for what they are. Detach from these instincts and from the need you feel that they must be for your survival.

The fear of abandonment is also predominant within the survival chakra. You feel there has to be something to keep you surviving, and you do not know what that is. Because this something is not known, it may abandon you at anytime creating fear for your existence, your survival.

Your physical existence also contains the intangibles of self-esteem and self-worth. Much of how you feel about yourself will reflect in your physical existence and flows through the survival chakra.

There are many types of fears related to survival that lie within this chakra as well as being a base for your instincts on the planet. Every thought, every interaction, every time you turn on the news, every movie you watch, whether you consider the movie to be real or not, forms perceptions that are stored within the chakras. Even your imagination affects the chakra system and is why creative visualization works. If the perception brings peace and harmony to you, it helps you to relax from your survival fears and instincts, but if you are watching somebody being threatened in a way that threatens you, that perception becomes strengthened. Imagine, lifetime after lifetime of perceptions being strengthened and stored in the survival chakra and how those perceptions limit you.

What happens when you clear these survival perceptions that for so long have defined your life on the planet? When you feel safe in your existence, you are then free to focus your attention on your existence from a spiritual standpoint. You begin to reflect upon your physical existence from your Divinity rather than reacting for your survival. Because the chakra system is interrelated, you may find you are freer to express in your throat, third-eye, and spiritual energy centers, for these are truly the ones that are your reality and create your existence for you.

Clearing the perceptions from the survival chakra will allow you to relate to the trees, flowers, animals, and the person who irritates you from a different perspective. To those people who you did not understand because you were afraid of them, you will open and see a beauty you missed before. You will feel more at peace about being physical. Thoughts of escaping the physical will diminish, and you will enjoy your physical existence more. You will discover a whole, new world!

8

****

SEXUAL / CREATIVITY CHAKRA

The second chakra is the chakra of sexuality and creativity located above the base chakra around the area of the naval. As you became physical, sexuality was deemed necessary for the continuing creation of physical existence. The only way you knew to bring forth life was through sexuality. Sexuality is also considered the only real form of creativity as you equate life with creativity. Procreation was your first creativity: the creation of physical bodies to house your soul, Spirit, and mental capabilities.

Realize there is a difference between creating and making. What you make comes from the analytical mind and the associated thought processes, but creating comes from the Divine mind creating what is from what is not. You make from known components, but you create from what does not exist.

As an example, you understand what goes into making life: chromosomes, eggs, sperm, etc. Those are the known components, but what makes a living being? What produces the personality or allows it to be a separate, functioning being? That is the creative part of bringing forth life from what is not and why sexuality and creativity are interwoven and placed together in this energy center.

How you view your sexuality and the resulting fears and limitations affect all of your creations and your whole creative force. If you have issues, such as guilt or pain about bringing children into the world from this lifetime or others, all of those issues and limitations are stored in this chakra. These limitations affect your creative ability, not only as you think of the creative pursuits of an artist, writer, or musician but also in your ability to create your life. When you are going through the mental process of creative visualization in attempting to bring about the things you desire, if the second chakra is blocked, you are then creating through the distortion of this chakra. Your creations will either take longer to manifest, or they will not come about the way you desire, or you may feel they do not come about at all.

Much of this chakra is clogged not only with your perception of sexual experiences but also with the fears of separation from Divinity. As you began to lose sight of your Divinity, you began to clog your sexuality storing the fear of the separation from the Creator within this energy center.

In your need to be safe, you have placed many parameters upon sexual behavior not only in this culture but also in cultures throughout human history. There have been many attempts to regulate sexual behavior thinking that if you could isolate it and make it pure you could once again identify with Divinity when actually the opposite is true. Thus the more you are able to free yourself from the guilt, fear, and pain, associated with sexual behavior, the more you will be able to express your Divinity. You will find the more you become spiritual, the greater will be your pleasure of sexuality. You will free yourself from the fear of not being a spiritual being and thereby, become freer to express the oneness of life. Sexuality is, therefore, more than just a means of procreation; it is the closest experience you can have with your Divinity and being one in a physical sense.

The ability to fully express in conjunction with the Divine mind working with your analytical abilities is how you would hold out your hand and produce an apple. The sexual/creativity chakra is very important to manifestation, but the perceptions of the experiences stored within the creativity portion of this chakra have long blocked the ability to express. For so long you have forsaken the conscious choice of creativity that this ability within the sexual/creativity chakra has become dormant. You have not allowed yourself to understand this vibration, and therefore it has not been activated or allowed to expand. You have created with your analytical mind and have focused your attention on that aspect rather than going through the Divine. Consequently, you have not fully used and benefited from the abilities within the creativity portion of this chakra.

To be able to manifest your desires, you must clear the fear of your creative powers stored within this chakra. It is not just the fear you are consciously aware of but also the fear from all of your experiences of all of your lifetimes related to your creative abilities that have clogged this chakra. All of the creations you have perceived as being painful have translated into fear that must be cleared and transformed. As you allow these fears to clear, you will begin to move into the ability of manifestation through expression.

Now, manifestation through expression is effortless. You do not have to work at it. You do not have to hold images or keep your thoughts focused in order to create. You think the thought, and it is manifested. This creative ability has been buried for so long that you do not know how to use it. You considered this ability to be a thousand years into the future rather than something you could use today.

As you begin to create through expression rather than through the analytical mind, you will begin to manifest purely and come to respect the power that resonates within you. You will recognize with unlimited power there is nothing you are lacking and therefore nothing to fear. You will begin to rest in the peace of the totality of who you are. When this chakra is clear, the ability to align with the Divine mind through your analytical mind and manifest your desires effortlessly rather than making them from the limitation of experiences is enhanced. The sexual/creativity chakra is key to once again developing this ability.

All of humanity is filled with blockages in this chakra resulting from what is perceived to be life on the planet. This chakra is connected more to your perception of your Divinity than to the perception of your creativity or your sexuality. As you clear this chakra, you will tie together sexuality with spirituality. You will recognize the sexual experience as more than physical and begin to experience it through your expression. Sexuality will become the totality of the essence of creativity, spirituality, and physical union. The element of the Divine will be brought into your experience, and if you are a creative person, an artist of any type, you will become freer, and your expression will begin to take on a quality of mastership.

9

****

THE EMOTIONAL CHAKRA

The emotional chakra is located between love (your heart chakra) and creativity (the sexual/creativity chakra) in your solar plexus. This chakra is one of the most powerful energy centers dealing with your ego and the lower three chakras, for the emotions affect the mind, your physical body, and for brief moments can even override the spiritual essence.

All of the emotions are in the emotional body. The emotional body has the knowledge of how the emotions can be activated to keep you safe from the ego perspective. You can think of the emotional body as the storehouse for the emotions being able to pull out frustration or anger whenever the emotion is triggered.

The emotional chakra is tightly connected to the emotional body. The emotional body acts like a sentinel on guard whereas the emotional chakra is the storehouse of the perceptions of the emotions. Now you might argue the perception has to go out to the emotional body for the emotional body to respond, and many times such is the case. But for the most part the emotional body reacts first and then the emotional chakra comes into play, but it is so instantaneous you would have difficulty determining which happens first.

Within the chakra system, the emotional chakra will process an experience before the other chakras. Whatever you are experiencing, whether you are frightened or in love, you will first experience it through the emotional chakra. The experience will impact the emotional body, flow into the emotional chakra, then distribute either up and/or down into the other chakras. The perception of your emotions reacting to what is taking place thus determines the affect on the other portions of your vibrational pattern.

Because there is a sense within your total being-ness that says you are not safe the emotions become activated. Perhaps this is in your survival chakra because the emotions and survival instincts are closely tied together. Or perhaps the sexual/creativity chakra says you have been attacked somehow resulting in your creativity being stifled. The emotional body then goes into action taking out of its storehouse the emotion it believes best protects you: anger, rejection, depression, etc. So the emotions can be triggered from the perceptions of any chakra within the chakra system. Once the emotional body is activated, of course, the emotional chakra then continually fills and stores the perception of what is taking place.

The emotional energy center collects all of the perceptions of your emotions. Even when you are dreaming, the emotional chakra continues to collect the perceptions of those particular experiences. Therefore, the subconscious mind, which dictates so many things beyond your conscious awareness, is very much affected by the emotional chakra.

Experiencing your emotions tells you if you are safe, and the fact that you need to know if you are safe tells you it is ego. For when you are in the Spirit and the reality of who you are you can only be safe. The emotions are the first line of defense for the ego system and therefore part of what is not.

The emotions are not something you should rid yourself of at this time. Your emotions are beautiful, for they are an expression of your feelings within the ego. If you did not have an emotional body as you moved into the ego, you would live life in a very cold, calculated, and non-experiential manner. That kind of a life would have little value to your soul.

The emotional chakra stores fear, for all emotions are fear-based. What you want to do is free yourself of the limitations stored in this energy center by healing and transforming all of your perceptions, fears, and blockages. This can be done because your creative power truly has power over the emotions.

The way to heal the limitations is through non-judgment and Love. Move beyond judging your emotions whether the emotion is anger, frustration, or what you perceive to be love; it does not matter. If you judge an emotion, you simply amplify the energy of the emotion, but by loving the emotion just as it is, you will defuse the limitation.

Feel the emotions without judgment and without resistance. Wrap the emotion with Love completely enveloping the emotion. You can use a visual picture, but it is best if you can feel it. Feel it; do not fight it! Do not be upset by your emotions or wish them away. Allow the emotions to stand without judgment and without guilt. For when you are afraid, you feel guilty about being afraid, and when you feel angry, you feel guilty about being angry.

Wrap your Love around your emotional body, and let Love penetrate into the emotions. Even if the love is the emotion of love, you will begin to feel safe as you experience the other emotions. As you begin to feel safe, call upon the part of you that is Divine. (Before this point you may not be willing to allow the Divine entrance.) Ask the Divine to move into the vibration of the emotion, and transform the vibration.

To transform the emotions, the steps are:

> ➤ Do not resist the emotions but allow them to stand without judgment or guilt. Resisting only holds the emotions in place thereby energizing, strengthening, and empowering them. The only reason you resist something is because you are afraid. Resistance powers the fear of the emotions.
> ➤ Embrace the emotions without judgment. Wrap the emotion with your love and *feel it.*
> ➤ Remove yourself from the process and move into the request or the intent of the Divine. You will not feel the Divine, but you will feel the result. When you allow the Divine Love to move in to heal and transform the limitations, you will feel the result, the peace, and the deep inner strength. Now you will be in a place of experiencing without the limitations of the emotions.

This is a very powerful exercise to free you from the limitation of your emotions.

Peace, joy, harmony, and Divine love are not emotions. An emotion may be happiness or the feeling of love you express through the emotions. Because the emotions greatly affect your physical body, it is important the emotional chakra be clear of limitations and fears. Clearing your vibrational pattern by moving into the transformational process allows the emotional chakra to process your experiences without distortion.

As you clear the emotional chakra, you will find a freedom also flows into the other chakras. The emotional chakra, more than any other chakra, determines how you live life and what you allow yourself to believe, try, or do. You can do anything, but the emotions are the sentinel on guard to say if it is safe. If you fell to your death from a high place and did it in total peace, you would have no fear of heights. Death is only transformation, and you have done that many times. It is the fear for the survival of your existence that affects the emotional center, and it is fear that dictates before anything else how your decisions will be made.

How the emotional body responds to the perceptions of your experiences stored within the emotional chakra is what limits you. Begin to clear those limitations thereby allowing your emotional body to heal and become a vessel for demonstrating the essence of your power, spirituality, and unlimited-ness. Until it does, there is no way you can move your vibration into the unlimited being you are choosing and preparing to be. These are important steps you can take in your own transformation and clearing your chakras is prime to your beginning.

10

****

THE HEART CHAKRA

At the seat or at the very "heart" of your vibrational pattern is the heart chakra. It is located in the area of the heart aligned along the spine. If you listen to your heart, you can move into your soul's awareness, for the soul connects to your vibrational pattern through the heart chakra. Therefore, listening to your heart chakra is the same as listening to your soul.

All of the other energy centers and cellular existence communicates with the heart chakra. The heart chakra aligns the other chakras becoming a base of control for the chakra system. As you center your intent on becoming All-That-Is, you are indeed clearing and aligning the heart chakra. The energy or vibrations within this chakra holds together the reality of your existence on the planet, for if it did not, you would not exist.

Energies of the lower three chakras and of the upper three chakras connect through the heart chakra. The basis of your physical existence (the lower three chakras) connects with your spiritual essence (the upper three chakras) in the center of Love within the heart chakra. While you may have an experience that creates a fear perception in your survival chakra, the third-eye chakra may give an insight bringing balance or peace to the fear through the heart chakra. The chakras are an integrated system whereby your perceptions do not flow into just one chakra, but some portion of the perception will touch into many of the chakras.

Love is All-That-Is, and the heart chakra is the connection between physical and spiritual allowing the two to manifest. It is impossible to exist outside of Love, for Love is the reality; Love sustains life, and the heart chakra is the center of Love.

The emotion of love resides in your emotional chakra, but the heart chakra contains your experiences of love on two levels: on the level of the emotions and on the level of your spirituality experiencing the all that you are. Because the emotion of love is fear, the heart chakra will contain fear, but there also is a part that has experienced your spirituality.

Most of the time you interpret love as having a secure feeling about something, but the experience of love can restrict you from giving and receiving love freely. Your experience has said love includes pain whether that was the loss of a loved one through: death, abandonment, or being forced to walk away from someone you loved. The experience contained pain, and the fear associated with that pain resides within the heart chakra because the ego system overrode the expression of Love.

The second component residing within the heart chakra is the expression of Love and that is pure reality. When you feel your heart swollen with Love, you are actually feeling the Love of the universe as it flows in and expresses through the emotions. The emotions are felt by every component of your body, but the heart, being the center of love, will feel Love the clearest.

Outside of experience the heart chakra is where expression radiates. This is where the expression of who you are and the reality of who you are resides. As you begin to express, experience will no longer be what you know and understand. You will understand expression. At this time you are preparing to express. This is a glorious journey not taken for a long time, and indeed, you have almost forgotten you are capable of such an undertaking. The heart chakra is very important in allowing this journey.

As with all of the other chakras, what you want to do is clear the fears so your expression can radiate through this energy center. You will find the heart chakra is one of the most difficult places to allow the fears to heal, for the heart chakra hits at the very autonomy of your ego system. Therefore, you may find more resistance than you anticipated in allowing the transformation to take place. However, you will know when it occurs because this is your road to unconditional love.

Unconditional love is the Love that exists no matter what is taking place. Unconditional love is Love without expectations and without judgment. Unconditional love is being able to Love the unlovable in your perception. This does not mean tolerate but Love and embrace.

If, for instance, someone came to your door who had not

bathed for a month, their breath smelled of all they had taken in, and they cursed and swore, you may find it difficult to say, "Come just as you are and sleep in my house tonight." You might be able to say, "Take a bath, clean up, put on clean clothes; you are going to have to meet my standards to enter my home." Then, of course, you do not love unconditionally. Find it in your heart to love people just as they are without judgment and without the need to change them in any way. That is unconditional love on a physical level.

To love unconditionally on an emotional level is to be emotionally unaffected by another person's emotions. Remember what is happening, an emotion is created from a person's perception of safety that you perceive attacks you. Can you Love this person not in spite of his or her attack but embracing the person just as he or she is? If you can, you will find total peace. You will find Love touches into the heart and does what you wanted anyway, not because you or the person planned it that way, for it is always up to the individual to recognize the Love within him or her.

It is not for anyone to set the standards of behavior in any manner upon another human being. By what right can you do this? Your value system comes from either society's value system or your own past experiences. It does not come from the Divine expression within, for the Divine expression within does not have a value system.

As the heart chakra clears, it is going to allow you to move to unconditional love. Unconditional love threatens the ego because unconditional love takes down all of the ego's defense mechanisms. Do not think that coming from unconditional love is something you cannot do. You can do this! Make peace with your ego system and bring it into harmony with the Divine within you. When you do, there will be a light about you that is undeniable—an inner light that flows through your entire vibrational pattern.

The heart chakra is blocked by your perceptions of rejection, pain, and hurt revolving around the emotion of love. This has nothing to do with the reality of unconditional love but has been formed by your perceptions of how you have experienced love on the planet. If, in your lifetimes, you have had a number of love rejections, abandonment, betrayals, or lack of trust, the heart chakra can become extremely blocked, and you may be unable to really Love. You are then unable to receive Love and are unable to give Love. Instead you function within a narrow range of exchange with your fellow human beings. You have determined your value by how you perceived the love from others. Your analysis and understanding of that love lead you to believe you are not good enough to be loved. You loved as deeply as you knew how and that love was betrayed. All of these perceptions enter into your heart chakra, clogging the chakra and result in a fear to Love.

Once you allow yourself to recognize the love from another is not needed to validate yourself, you will begin to feel safe enough to open, give, and receive Love.

Understand each soul on the planet loves to the extent allowed by the blockages within the heart chakra and is simply attempting to heal the pain. Your encounter with another soul means you have chosen each other in which to do this. Many times what you perceive to be rejection, hurt, or pain is because of something totally unrelated to you. When you are afraid to open (you may not consciously be aware of this), the blockages can increase and the pain can reach a point where you are no longer able to continue the relationship. One person or the other will find a means to push the other person away and then this cycle will repeat again.

Recognize the validation of your worth and power is separate from the relationship. You are total and complete within yourself and do not need the validation of another. Each relationship in your life you chose, be it a parent, a friend, a boss, or intimate lover, as an opportunity to heal the pain within yourself as others also chose these relationships for healing. You are not responsible for how each person chooses to interact within a relationship, but you are responsible for how you choose to act and whether you choose to take advantage of the opportunity provided to heal.

Realize you have pain and blockages from past experiences stored within the heart chakra and at this point you are not capable of giving and receiving love as freely as you could.

Realize to Love means to Love without expectation, giving your Love freely expecting nothing in return, opening to receive Love knowing it is safe if tomorrow Love is not there. These are two big hurdles for humanity: to Love without expectation of anything in return, and to receive Love knowing it is safe if it is gone tomorrow. These are active choices always available for you to make.

As you make these choices and allow the blockages to clear, you will enter a dimension of life with such an understanding and awareness of humanity that you can enjoy others no matter how they irritate or hurt you. You will see their pain but also their beauty. Your Love flows freely to them without conditions and expectations and soon the relationships begin to shift, and you have not even tried to make a shift. You begin to feel people are warmer and nicer because your Love has activated their Love helping them to heal. With Love there is no struggle: only peace, beauty, and safety.

11

****

THE THROAT CHAKRA

Experience is connected with the lower three chakras and everything you have chosen to manifest and place in linear time. How you relate through the perception of those manifestations dictates what your experience will be. All of the information, feelings, and emotions from these experiences are stored and available for making decisions.

The true power of the throat chakra lies in expression and has nothing to do with experience; yet the wonderful, latent ability of this chakra has been used to create from experience. As you choose to create from the analytical mind, the data from all of your perceptions of your manifestations come through the power of the throat chakra dominating your creative process. Thus the throat chakra has become like a tightly clogged drain letting only drips of expression through rather than flowing.

Expression is manifesting in the All-That-Is, truly allowing your creative powers to manifest without limitations, attachments, or judgment—just allowing the expression to flow. When you express, you no longer feel the emotions of anger, resentment, depression, or upset because you are not attached to those things. Power is not given to those things that trigger your emotions from the perceptions of your creations called experience. As you express, you begin to see the true power of creation, and your true creative powers come through.

Humanity has a tendency to try to use this power from their experience rather than from expression. That is attempting to use the power from the ego, which is impossible, for one is still viewing life from the perspective of need, judgment, and limitation, and therefore not expressing.

Expression is difficult to understand because your mind is analytical and part of the experience; therefore, to express requires trusting in your Divinity. You have to trust you are the expression of an unlimited, creative source that is total and complete. You are an extension of this power and only have to allow this power of Divinity to express. The first way you will know you are allowing the power of your Divinity to express is through the throat chakra, for the throat chakra is the center of expression and will located in the throat area of the body.

The throat chakra is the center that allows the expression of your creative power. You have distorted this source of expression and now you are expressing in a limited manner but still expressing, which is still your clearest power of your spiritual essence. (See authors note at end of chapter.) In reality Love is the power, and Love is All-That-Is (all means inclusive). Love loves yourself for expressing as you are now. You must remove the judgment of expressing from your experience in order to allow the process of expression to begin.

As previously stated, expression is difficult because it cannot happen through the analytical mind. You can do many things with the ego system, but you will never be able to hold out your hand and manifest a loaf of bread, for the ego is incapable of such creations. The ego believes in separation, and as long as the loaf of bread is separate from you, you cannot produce it. You have to believe the loaf of bread is already within you to bring it forth. That is why removing your attachments, judgments, and limitations are so important. You attempt to make it work through your analytical mind and it cannot. The mind cannot see how this could work because the ego belief system says it cannot, and that makes it difficult for you to trust your Divinity enough to find out what happens. The more you surrender everyday to your Divinity, the more you see the miracles flow in your life, but miracles are not produced through the analytical mind or your experiences.

The throat chakra is your center for bringing forth your expression into the third-dimensional world. The power pack behind the expression of your creative force in the world is your will. Your will is connected and centered within your Divinity—that being your soul to your Spirit and therefore your will is always in alignment with your highest and best journey in this world.

You may have encountered someone who has come to the planet with a strong purpose and knows what it is he or she desires to accomplish in life. The center of will and expression is the vehicle that will bring this purpose into being.

Sometimes as a child or an adult the person will not feel on equal footing with those in authority, and the power pack of will can be diminished, even though this person came with a clear understanding of what it was here to express.

Why does this happen? Because the path the soul knows it needs to follow is not in harmony with the perceptions of those around the soul. Attempts are made to bring the soul in line so those in authority are more at peace with themselves. This often perpetuates the pain on the planet, for these souls could truly lead your world if they were allowed but rather they are made to conform to the pain. The will being the power driving the expression is quickly disconnected resulting in more confusion than direction. This is often what you call a broken Spirit or broken will.

Children will often freely sing, and yet by the time of adulthood, their expression is so diminished they sing no more. What could have developed into a beautiful vocal cord for singing and expansive expression, instead, diminishes. Every soul on the planet should have a beautiful, singing voice.

For the most part you come to the planet very connected to your power pack, the soul and the Spirit. As you begin to grow, you find your will, which powers your expression, is not always pleasing to others. Your will does not align with their pain and consequently, there is an attempt to align your expression with the pain of others.

As an example, take the expression of a group of souls who demonstrate for what thcy feel to be their world connection, but their expression does not align with the established order of society. How often is that expression squelched? Yet, there may have been something that could have enhanced every soul on the planet. Everyone has experienced this in one way or the other, whether you are a rebel with a cause, or whether you thought the easiest way to live was to diminish yourself to avoid chaos in your life. Whichever way you have chosen does not matter, for your power of expression has to some extent conformed to the ego process of safety. As you conformed, you blocked your expression and placed blockages within the throat chakra.

So what happens? You no longer remember how to express the beautiful you that you are. The total picture of who you are no longer aligns with the survival instincts that are perceived to be in your best interest. As you begin to clear these blockages, you are going to discover an expressive part of you long buried. You are going to open a new avenue of existence for yourself and the planet. This is how you will take the first steps toward becoming the Masters of the creative essence that you are, for until you take back the clarity of expression, you cannot truly bring into existence what your heart desires to its fullest extent.

One of the truest expressions on the planet is sound, so is it any wonder you find so many problems with the throat. Have you ever noticed on days when your throat seems clearer, your voice is richer and fuller? Do you think something happened to your vocal chords? Those were the days you cleared a few blockages or you expressed a little more fully from the vibrations that are not blocked. On other days your voice is not clear, and you struggle with expressing. All of this pertains to the throat chakra.

To be the expressive, beautiful you that your soul truly is, you must clear the blockages from the throat chakra. As you clear your throat chakra, you will find your voice will change. Your range of sound will become larger and clearer. Notice these things as you begin to work and clear your throat chakra.

From your throat chakra your expression creates. You may find you have more conflict within you as you clear your throat chakra because as your expression flows more freely, it conflicts with the old ways of experience. A part of your "will" is torn between trusting your expression and the safety of the ego system. Your mind will have a difficult time with this because it is at the very core of how you create on the planet. Divinity must flow through everything to keep it in existence, but you are not creating from Divinity and expression. When you begin to clear the throat chakra, it will give you more access to expression.

The conflict between experience and expression is the same as the conflict between illusion and reality—Love and fear. The conflict never lies with reality, Love, or expression. The conflict is always on the ego side of illusion, fear, and experience; it is only there because you are frightened in attempting to maintain your existence in a safe environment. At these times it is important to recognize what the ego is and why you created it.

So you have choices. If your fear does not allow you to move into Love, reality, and expression, you shall continue to live from experience. You will continue to live from the ego system with only what you know to be your perception of reality. But it is not your reality, instead it is your perception of reality. You must trust you are safe outside of the mechanisms of the ego, the attacks, your emotions, and fears.

Get in touch with your Divinity—not with the ego, or how you feel about something, or what your experience says to you. Get in touch with that place of peace, joy, harmony, and true Love. Get in touch with the place that allows you to believe you are All-That-Is—the place within you that believes everything exists and is the reason why you can manifest. When you move into this place, take action by allowing the flow of those expressions. Know when the expressions begin to flow. Experience may well wish to stop the expression because experience says you cannot do that; it is not safe.

Again you have choices. Do you follow experience and your analytical mind or do you follow the flow of expression? Now that is not easy because you live in the real world, and you have decisions to make. How do you make decisions if you do not do it from experience? The answer is you do not have to make decisions, and you will not be making decisions if you come from expression. You will be flowing with your existence as you speak words in a very natural process. If you allow yourself to express, it will be like going from struggle to the depths of immortality, spaciousness, and vastness beyond what your mind can comprehend—truly beyond!

Authors note: The abilities of the sexual creativity chakra (chapter 8) and the throat chakra go hand in hand in many respects. As has been stated before, the chakras are very interrelated. The sexual/creativity chakra by itself does not have the ability to create from nothing. It takes the will and expression of the throat chakra to really make this happen. The perceptions and fears of separation from Divinity and of your creative powers stored within the sexual/creativity chakra tend to also block the expression of these abilities within the throat chakra. In order, therefore, to truly manifest from nothing requires both of these chakras be clear.

Expression has been defined as experiencing without limitation. In a convoluted sense, experiencing with limitation is within the realm of all-possibilities and can be considered a form of expression albeit a limited form of expression. Experiencing in a limited manner is a form of expression if you are aware and know you are choosing to express in a limited manner from the vastness of all-possibilities. In other words you are not trapped in the limitation.

12

****

THE THIRD-EYE CHAKRA

The third-eye chakra is aptly named because it is located in the middle of your forehead. This energy center is focused in this area of the body to override the mind, but so much power has been given to the analytical mind it has instead enveloped the third-eye chakra.

The third-eye chakra should be your source of information as it enters your vibrational pattern and disseminates through your mental capacities for use in your everyday life. Instead you have substituted the ego system that primarily utilizes emotions for determining your everyday existence. The emotions have become your barometer for determining if you are safe. By allowing the emotions to become dominant, the third-eye chakra (which has no emotions or emotional barometer) has been by-passed, and the emotions have moved directly into the mental and physical bodies.

How has this affected you? The affect has been to diminish your connection with your Divine source thereby losing a tremendous ability of expansion, creativity, and awareness of who you are. This connection from Spirit, to soul, to third-eye, to mind has instead become for the most part just mind.

This is the extreme case. There are times you allow the flow of information to come into the third-eye chakra, and you trust and go with it because it feels right to you. You are then coming from that intuitive, inner knowing, Spirit connection. At other times you override this information because your analytical mind and emotions say the information cannot be trusted, and you will not be safe. You then live from the ego system rather than trusting in the Divine power that you are.

All of the chakras are joined and aligned, but the third-eye chakra and the crown chakra are joined to a higher degree allowing the spiritual essence to come primarily through the third-eye chakra. The third-eye chakra does not bring understanding but knowing. Knowing is different from understanding. To understand something you must have the components of the problem and the data for the analytical mind to analyze so that your questions can be answered and understood. But you cannot understand knowing. Knowing goes far beyond understanding.

Knowing is something you cannot rationalize or necessarily explain to the neighbor next-door. When the neighbor thinks you are crazy for what you are doing, all you can say is you just know this is right. You are unable to say, "Look, I have all of this data that will make you understand why I am doing this." That is not the process of knowing.

You follow knowing because you recognize if you do not, you are settling for less than best. Understanding has grades and scales but knowing has no such scale. Knowing is following something without question because you know that you know that you know.

Revelations come as knowing. A revelation is something you cannot necessarily explain; you did not read what the revelation contains from a book or have data to prove it, but suddenly you knew it was true. Everyone has had experiences like this, but they may have been small, scattered, or dismissed.

Opening the third-eye is about living from knowing instead of understanding. It is about inner trust; it is going beyond the ego system of fear and knowing you are a spiritual being who can live in harmony with All-That-Is. To live in harmony with All-That-Is means to live without prejudice, judgment, attachments or needs. You are aware there is beautiful music to life and recognize you are a vibration in the melody of life that is in sync with All-That-Is. You have no reason for fear, struggle, or strife; therefore, you have no need to understand before stepping forth with knowing in your life. As long as you have the need to understand, you are coming from the ego, and you will have difficulty recognizing your vibration in the melody of life.

To open and receive through the third-eye chakra requires setting your intent and knowing this is truly your choice for your life. You desire to live from the awareness of the spiritual essence of who you are by no longer accepting to live in fear, worry, restriction, and limitation. Instead knowing you are eternally safe in your existence and have Divine guidance that says you are on your soul's path. That is what you came to do in this lifetime and all of this must flow through the third-eye chakra.

To suddenly open the third-eye chakra and know everything is not likely; there are stages to opening this chakra. The ego will certainly try to convince you that you are committing a form of suicide and in many ways you are, for you are bringing to life a new source within you long forgotten. Life becomes an expression that is like walking through a beautiful garden having a variety of flowers you have never seen before—each more beautiful than the other. It is a different way of living. It is living in trust, flowing, and having new revelations pour into you and not fighting those revelations. Your resistance to these things is what creates your problems.

When you take this journey into the spiritual world of knowing through your third-eye chakra, you create a new world of love, beauty, harmony, and joy. But you will never get there through the mind that needs to understand. This new life can only come about through knowing and opening the third-eye chakra will hasten it. The third-eye chakra will help and assist you, but it begins by removing the blockages that keep you from knowing. The ego system has locked this away because the ego thinks it does not work for you. As you remove the blockages (by clearing the chakras), you are going to flow in your life. You only need to trust. Your spiritual essence connected to All-That-Is brings to your consciousness this knowing, trust, and awareness.

13

****

THE CROWN CHAKRA

The seventh chakra, or the spiritual, crown chakra, is an energy center not quite like any of the other energy centers, for there is not an energy center for your spirituality. How could there be? Everything you are is spiritual. Spirituality is certainly not confined or limited to one small place, but you focus the energy or vibration of spirituality into this particular spot within your vibrational pattern. This is the place where you allow the connection with the higher part of yourself, the angels, the Love of the universe, and the higher power you perceive to be Divinity. You needed a place to bring this power into your vibrational pattern and the crown chakra serves that purpose, but it functions more like a gateway than an energy center.

For the moment, remove your concepts and judgment of

what is spiritual. Spiritual is All-That-Is, and it is through this spiritual gateway you connect by intent, desire and choice to what is. But your response to what you have connected to, through the spiritual chakra, is determined by the perceptions of your experiences.

Sometimes your vibrational pattern is so clogged with your experiences of fear you are unable to obtain a clear pathway or connection into Love. You then wonder why you have difficulty finding peace, harmony, or being able to connect to the angels of light and Love.

There are those who perceive they connect with darkness or demons, but it is the fear latent within their experiences that determines this connection to be of darkness. You could connect to the same vibration with your power of Love and never perceive the darkness others perceive through their fears. You might perceive pain, or a painful feeling, but your Love would quickly heal and send light to the fear vibrations.

Recognize your spiritual gateway allows you to connect to whatever is, but it is your perception that defines what this connection means to you.

If you feel safe, if you feel Love, if you feel your life will be enhanced for the better, your perceptions will say this is good. But if you feel fear in any way, your perceptions will lead you to conclude the experience is evil, dark, etc. You are just connecting to an experienced event in which you are placing a value system or judgment.

If the fears of past lives, this life, and childhood teachings say there are things "out there" that can get you, then your vibrational pattern can clog with fear. When you connect to anything you perceive falls into this category, your fears are triggered and amplified, and you become more fearful, but this is not because there is anything out there that can harm you.

Now, neither can anything out there save you. When it is said the angels or your spirit guides help you, they are really helping to amplify your Divinity. The power is in you. The angels just pull the curtain aside allowing the power within you to come forth to protect, heal, and keep you safe. Likewise when you connect with fear, your fear is amplified and becomes more of a reality to you. Your ego will say, "See I told you this is not a safe place."

You are an individualized expression of Divinity having many connections to all expressions and all creations. It is how you interpret those connections that determines if you move into fear or into Love and how you perceive your experiences on the planet. Recognize the spiritual chakra is a gateway of connection to All-That-Is. Spiritual is not defined by good nor bad. Spiritual is defined as Spirit and that is All-That-Is, all creation, and all processes—Divinity. Divinity is All-That-Is. It is your perception of what you have experienced and how you allow the fears to gather or be healed that amplifies the power within you of: ego or reality, fear or Love.

As you begin to shift from experience to expression, it is important to recognize the power is you. All that is triggered is you. Fear has no power. Fear only has the power you allow it to have. Nobody can do anything to you. The vibration of fear can only trigger what is within you. When you feel unsafe for whatever reason, connect the Energy Pathways to all of the chakras, and let the Love flow in and heal the fear.

It is time to recognize there is nothing of which to be

afraid and begin to live in the fullness of your Divine expression and the beauty of this world you have created. Physical existence is a beautiful, outward expression of unlimited freewill and creative ability inherent with life on this planet. When you move into Divinity and feel it, live it, you will realize the all-inclusive beauty of your expression and have no desire to leave this existence. As you move into the Divinity and the beauty, you will begin to clear your fears reflected upon the planet, and your world will become more beautiful.

The planet is beautiful, you are beautiful: see your planet with inner light glowing from all existence; harmony and music like you have never known; flowers like you have long forgotten; thoughts so pure and Divine it does not matter that all can read your mind. Without fear you are open to only Love and Divine expression.

This spiritual energy center or gateway can never be totally distorted, for it is actually the truth of who you are; the spiritual essence is who you are. The rest is what you have created and developed with the power of that spirituality. Many of those creations have become distorted by your perceptions of fears, survival, separation, and safety, but when you work with the chakra of your spiritual essence, know there is a part of it that will always remain pure and intact.

You cloud the ability of this gateway to connect with the spirituality of all life, and the Divinity existing in every creation. You cloud the connection to your own higher self, the angelic kingdom and the Creative Source. You limit the ability of this spiritual energy center to connect and bring into your consciousness the awareness of the Divine essence of All-That-Is.

The purpose of working with the spiritual chakra is not to change the energy pattern or essence of what is but to clear away the debris and blockages keeping you from being consciously aware of the spiritual connection you have with all life.

The spiritual chakra empowers all of the other energy centers. You are continually receiving the life force that always flows from the spiritual chakra and nothing can stop it. Even when you vacate the body, your vibrational pattern does not dissipate but stays intact. Chakras contain all of your experiences from all of your lifetimes because the energy pattern is intact even though it is no longer in the physical body. It is still in the essence of your soul. Your vibrational pattern is still vitalized and energized from the spiritual essence or the crown chakra as you know it in the physical body. It is important to realize nothing stops that flow.

There is no way you can shut off your spirituality, but you can shut it off from your conscious awareness. It is always your choice to consciously connect to or disconnect from your Divinity.

The third-eye chakra is important because it acts as an intermediary between the spiritual crown chakra and the rest of your vibrational pattern. Awareness from the spiritual chakra is brought into your consciousness by the third-eye chakra going beyond what your five senses can describe. The spiritual chakra is always operating through the third-eye chakra allowing the vibrations and awareness to flow to the other energy centers. Vibrations flow from the spiritual crown chakra into the other chakra centers and then out into the rest of your vibrational pattern.

Remember the chakra system filters the vibrations from the spiritual gateway causing distortion. Distortion is present because all of the perceptions of past experiences cloud the reality of who you are and your power. The more you clear the chakras, the purer or less distorted the spiritual vibrations will be flowing throughout your vibrational pattern, and the more empowered you will become.

As you begin to understand you are an unlimited being and how free you truly are, you will have no parameters and no boundaries. It will be a new existence for the expression of your creative power in the physical world, but you may have to find your way to allow the ego to be comfortable and safe with this new freedom.

Have you ever seen a person who, or an animal that has lived within limited physical or emotional parameters suddenly have these barriers removed? Was the person or animal able to immediately expand into their new freedom— knowing how to operate within the new parameters of their environment? Likely not, for they have only known what happens from their decisions and actions that created pain within the old environment. Therefore, the person or animal must first find their way and become accustom to the new environment, otherwise, they may be afraid to take responsibility for the creative process afforded by their new freedom.

When it is stated you will experience more freedom from clearing the chakras, be aware you may also find yourself in a place of having to walk gently through the new freedom until you become accustomed to the new power. It is as though you were chiseling in stone, and now suddenly you have a laser beam that creates faster. Your creative process speeds up, and your thoughts manifest faster. In clearing your chakras, you will find newfound freedom and empowerment within yourself. Recognize you are safe while experiencing this new freedom and power.

What if you do make a mistake? You will be able to recognize it, change course, and move beyond it. Realize this is an expansion of your awareness of who you are with less limitation and restriction.

Begin to live your life from Love. If you stay in a place of Love, you will find there is nothing to fear. The more freedom you have, with less limitations and restrictions, the more you need to come from Love. Let Love be your guiding light.

With every thought, every action, every desire, first stop and ask, "Am I in my center of Love?" If you are, you will find safety with your new freedom, and you will see the beauty of this new creative source. This is where you are going. How fast and on what road is in your hands, but you are moving to a day of true spiritual empowerment and awareness. All you have to do is remove some of the debris in your vibrational pattern placed there from the fear of the perception of separation. As the debris is cleared, empowerment increases, and you will begin to know what has been stated. You may not have total recognition at this moment, but as it begins to become your expression and your experience, you will know within you the truth of what is said.

You are an unlimited, spiritual being with a part of your existence focused in a physical, third-dimensional expression. Physical existence can be beautiful, wonderful, and harmonious. Living in peace, joy, and abundance can be yours. There is not a need for lack, but you have to be comfortable with abundance. You have not been accustomed to abundance as a way of life. Self-inflicted lack, pain, and punishment with brief moments of rewards squeezed in between is what you are used to, but consistent abundance in every area is a brand-new way of life. Yet, the spiritual energy from the spiritual chakra empowers abundance, freeing it, bringing to you beauty, Love, joy, and fulfillment.

The spiritual chakra is not magical, but it is a gateway to All-That-Is. Paying attention to what you bring forth and amplify within you is a beautiful tool to let you know if you are healing your fears and lighting your life no matter what road you travel or what comes your way.

EPILOGUE
✳✳✳✳✳✳✳

As consciousness first created and evolved into the physical dimension, life was experienced without limitation. The chakras were created for the sole purpose of defining experience and allowing expression within the physical dimension. At that point in the evolution of consciousness in the physical, perceptions and fear were not something stored within the chakra system.

As the consciousness of humanity began to believe in the separation from the source, the Creator, and began to process experiences in linear time, perceptions came about from the analysis of experiences to determine safety. Since the chakras were already involved with the process of defining experiences, the chakras became a natural place for storing the perceptions of those experiences coming from the ego system's approach to dealing with life and that became limiting.

The lower three chakras are more involved in storing the perceptions of physical experience. The upper three chakras, which deal more with your expression and connection to the spiritual essence, became distorted in part through how the lower chakras processed experience through perceptions and the beliefs that resulted. Remember the chakras are a system in which no one chakra is isolated but are instead interrelated.

When the chakras originally defined experience without limitation, they defined experience in what you may think of as a very neutral way. The chakras were used to define tangible aspects of experience such as grass and water to say sight in the third-eye and intangibles such as Love in the heart chakra. Qualities of expression through the chakras would include creativity in the sexual/creativity chakra, unconditional love in the heart chakra, and will in the throat chakra. All of these characteristics deal with your ability to express in the physical but not from limitation. That was the original purpose of the chakras and those abilities are still a part of the chakras today. The chakras only have to be cleared to free these abilities allowing the chakras to function again in a way that brings a richness and fullness to life. As the clearing happens, some very dramatic changes will occur within the chakras.

For instance, instead of the perceptions within the emotional chakra being used to feed the emotions of the ego system and again store the resulting perceptions of those experiences, the emotional chakra will be used to "feel" existence. Feeling is very different from living through the emotions. Feeling is not reactive. Feeling is about being alive and taking in every nuance of an experience so the experience can be fully lived. The third chakra could then be called the feeling chakra instead of the emotional chakra, but the use of the chakra will be very different without the affect of the perceptions.

In the appendix you will find a table of key chakra characteristics you can refer to from time to time to help refresh your memory. Also in the appendix is a glossary. At times, you have probably noticed, the use of some words are defined differently in the Salem vernacular, therefore it was felt a glossary would be helpful.

Clearing the chakras is an effective tool for reducing the perception load within the chakra system, but it cannot necessarily prevent the storing of more perceptions formed from the judgments you choose to make everyday. Therefore, choosing to practice the spiritual principles, such as non-judgment as outlined in chapter three, together with clearing the chakras further enhances the transformational process necessary to evolve the ego system and free oneself from the affects of the perceptions on one's life. It is a circular process, for by clearing the perceptions from the chakras, practicing and incorporating the spiritual principles in one's life is made easier. Clearing the chakras, therefore, is a powerful tool having many beneficial affects, which can be used by anyone choosing to free oneself from limitation and once again express from the reality of who you truly are.

Hopefully at this point, you can begin to see why clearing and working with the chakra system is key to help free you from the limitation and fear of the ego system, thereby opening the possibilities in your life. This book has focused mainly on the chakra system, but the chakras are only one tool that can be used to help expand your consciousness and become more spiritually self-aware. For instance, meditating and living the spiritual principles (as mentioned above) are other tools that can be applied and together can lift one up by the bootstraps so-to-speak to evolve the ego belief system and once again remember who you are.

It is your choice to decide if you want to evolve the ego system or not. This planet is a freewill planet and not everyone may be willing or wanting to make the choice of living life in a different manner by evolving the ego system. You may actually like the ego system, living on the edge, and feeling fear. The ego may have convinced you this is the best way to experience this planet. You have lived from the ego system for so long that undoubtedly you have had some good times doing it. What this all boils down to is there is a choice to be made, for it is not a given that you really desire to live beyond the ego system.

Now your Spirit understands this, and your soul probably recognizes evolving the ego is a better way to be, but you are primarily living from your ego system. Until you think there is a better way to do it, you may dabble a little bit here, you may change a few things there, and you may find all of this to be interesting information, but you may not want to live it. There must be a strong desire to let go of the ego processes and move into releasing your judgments, letting go of your attachments, living in the now-moment, clearing the chakras and doing all of the things having been spoken about in this book. That is when everything works together and becomes very effective.

Because the chakras play such a key role in how life is experienced within the physical, and clearing the chakras has such a powerful, beneficial affect in allowing life to be lived in a fuller, richer manner, this book was primarily devoted to the chakra system. Salem's teachings that describe in depth the broader scope of who we are, how we arrived at where we are today in our evolution, along with where we could go as a species, and other tools that can be of benefit to one's spiritual journey will be left for other works that are in process*. It is my sincere hope you are able to find the information in this book helpful in opening the possibilities in your life leading to a richer, fuller life for you and humanity. May your path be blessed as you journey on the planet with everyone who has chosen to be a part of the physical experience. Journey well and always remember to ask for help along the way!

*If you are interested in knowing when other works in the Path To Remembrance series becomes available, you can visit www.PathToRemembrance.com or call toll free 1-866-877-6992 or send in the quick order form in the back of this book to be placed on a notification list.

*"The path to Divinity is not through the
understanding of your analytical mind;
rather, it is a matter of listening to yourself,
trusting yourself, and knowing you are safe
as you begin to change your vibrational
pattern."*

Appendix

Characteristics of the Chakras

	Chakra	Location	Governs	Effect of Clearing	Key To:
Experience Lower Chakras Physical Existence	**Base/Survival** (Red)	Base of Spine	Survival & Survival Instincts	Frees the expression of the upper chakras, allows a view of existence from a spiritual perspective	Freedom from survival concerns & limitations
	Sexual/Creativity (Orange)	Naval	Sexuality, Creativity, Separation from Divinity	Unity of creativity, spirituality, & physical union	Manifesting & allowing the Divine into experience
	Emotional (Yellow)	Solar Plexus	Emotions	Removing fear	Expanding possibilities
Connects Upper & Lower Three Chakras	**Heart** (Green)	Heart	Love, Connection to the Soul	Movement toward unconditional love	Unconditional Love
	Throat (Blue)	Throat	Will & Expression	Frees expression and the connection of the will to the source	The flow of expression & the power of will in the physical
Expression Upper Chakras Spiritual Essence	**Third-Eye** (Indigo)	Forehead	Knowing, dissemination of spiritual awareness	Improved flow of awareness to the other energy centers	Living from knowing rather than understanding
	Crown/Spiritual (Violet)	Top of Head	Gateway to what is, the spiritual essence, All-That-Is	Undistorted connection to the spiritual essence	Connecting to the spiritual essence

127

Questions

In this appendix are questions asked of Salem during several chakra workshops given by Diandra on various occasions. You may find within this appendix a same or similiar question to the ones you may have and benefit from the answers given either directly or indirectly. These questions and answers are included as another means to further understanding and clarify the information on the chakras.

Questions – General

Q: *Do ascended masters and angels have chakras?*

A: The angels do not have a chakra system. They have a much different vibrational pattern, and their purpose does not involve a need for a chakra system.

As for the ascended masters, they have experienced life on the planet and therefore have created a chakra system. But the chakra system of an ascended master is not the same as the chakra system you know. When you reach the vibrational level of an ascended master, your chakra system will no longer need to perform the functions in the same manner as your chakra system does today. Your chakra system will be transformed to contain experiences of a different nature and therefore will be used for a different purpose. The chakra system will be modified to contain the experiences at the levels of an ascended master.

Q: *It has been stated clearing the chakras will help one to*

express rather than live from experience. Living from experi-
ence is also connected with analyzing experiences in linear
time. My question is can you not express if you place experi-
ences in linear time?

A: Yes you can express and place experiences in linear time.
You can do anything if you are expressing. The difference is
expression means you know you are all-possibilities. You
know you have the right of passage in any dimension you
want to move into, outside of time or inside of time. You can
still experience, but you are living the experience in a way
that is not limiting. When you live from expression, you are
simply living without limitation. Meaning anything is possible you believe is possible and choose to be possible.

Understand if you are living from expression even in linear
time, it will be different from living in your limitation because
you are seeing and living every nuance of every second of
every moment in its richness and fullness in expression. When
you are living the experience of linear time from limitation,
you are mostly surviving it. What do we mean by that? We do
not mean you are always in danger, but you are surviving one
moment to get to the next moment, to the next moment, to
the next moment, whether those moments are pleasurable or
not to you.

When living from expression, you are never in survival.
From expression you can still choose to have the experience
of linear time, but you know you are much more, and what
you are living is just a choice at that moment of experience.

Questions – Survival Chakra

Q: *Does the fear of heights have anything to do with the survival chakra?*

A: Yes, it is very much located in this chakra. Undoubtedly placed there by a past experience at sometime creating the fear.

Q: *Are the physical limitations placed on our bodies, like hunger and pain, related to the survival chakra?*

A: Only in the sense of how you perceive physical to be. For some people food is extremely important and for other people it is totally unimportant. For some individuals pain is something that is very frightening and for other individuals there is an actual thrill to a certain amount of pain. So it is your perception of the physical experience as to what kind of vibration it creates in the chakra system. Remember, it is always your perception of the experience and not the experience itself that causes the pain. It is the perception of the experience that becomes stored within the chakras.

Questions – Sexual/Creative Chakra

Q: *Can you give an example of what may manifest in our lives if the sexual/creativity chakra were totally clear?*

A: Anything. Anything, because if the sexual/creativity chakra were totally clear you would have no desire to manifest something that would be of harm to anyone or anything—be that-tangible or intangible. For the sexual/creativity chakra to be totally clear will require you to be at a totally different place spiritually. Thus you could manifest anything you desired. If you needed a shade tree, you would speak it into existence, or if a storm raged, you would quiet it if you chose. But you would have the wisdom to know when to do that. Your spiritual connection would be so deep you would probably have the need to manifest very little.

Q: *Can you give an example of how blockages relate to the second chakra?*

A: All of the lifetimes of experience you have had with your creativity since you believed you were separated are stored within this chakra. Very few vibrational patterns within humanity have the clarity and understanding of true oneness without fear. So for you to say I am going to manifest a loaf of bread tomorrow may not be likely. It is a process of recognizing and clearing, then allowing the expressive, creative ability to begin to take over and step out of your fears. The first fear you have to step out of is your fear of survival. As long as you have fears of survival, they are certainly going to affect your creativity and sexual chakra.

With respect to the sexual aspect of this chakra, the blockages are much the same. You are experiencing sex from your experiences of fear and joy. If you died in some lifetime giving birth, you may have a great fear of becoming pregnant. Many, many things of which you do not have a conscious awareness related to this chakra could affect and hold you in limitation. Your puritan background or culture having strict rules on sex can create blockages within this center. All of these things affect this chakra, and you do not have to know what they are. You just have to be willing to clear them out bit by bit.

Q: *Is there a particular tone that can be used to break through blockages within the chakras such as a sound, a vowel, or a consonant?*

A: Sound is extremely important, and just as you move up the musical scale, you can use sound to move vibrations within your chakra system. Now, because the chakras are so inter- woven with each other it is not quite as simple as moving up the musical scale. But if you just simply sing, hum, or form your musical scale, it is a very beautiful way of bringing sound to help you align the energy or vibrations within the chakras. Sound is your creative power; thus, sound is important and can be used to help move the vibrations.

Q: *Is there a benefit to directing energy to a particular chakra such as through the healing energy of therapeutic touch?*

A: Yes, and because everything experienced in the minor chakras flood into the major chakras the benefit could be more extensive. Yes.

Q: *When we took on the limitations of other universes, are these limitations stored in the chakras or does it go deeper than that? For example, a tree in another universe could not stand up and walk away; therefore, in this universe of unlim- ited freewill we assume that a tree cannot stand up and walk away.*

A: The chakras contain the perceptions of your experiences. I do not know that I could limit your example to just your chakras because the chakras are part of your creation as a human soul and what you speak of goes beyond that. But it would affect your perception of experiences on this planet. Yes.

Questions – Emotional Chakra

Q: *Is the emotional chakra the center to focus on for removing memory blocks?*

A: The energy centers themselves do not contain definitive memories of experience. They contain the perception of the experience. The experience itself is in various parts of your cellular memory, mental and emotional bodies. All of your perceptions of those experiences flow into these energy centers to help evaluate an experience and determine how you want to handle the next one that comes along.

With respect to memory blocks, you may find you no longer have a burning need to remember if the blockage of the perception is gone, or you may find that without the blockages your memory is very clear. All of the chakras may affect this, (not just one), but the emotional chakra is certainly very powerful in all of your ego-based experiences.

Q: *What is Divine? Is golden light Divine?*

A: If golden light represents the Divine to you, then yes it is Divine. Whatever represents Divinity to you is Divine. But remember Divinity is not an emotion and therefore is not something you feel. What will happen as a result of bringing in the Divine, which may happen in minutes, hours or maybe days, is you will begin to feel peace and a flow you did not have before, for you are removing the limitations of your fears.

Q: *Can you differentiate between the emotions and spiritual experiences of joy, harmony, or oneness?*

A: The best way to differentiate between spiritual experiences and the emotions at this time is if your experinece is free of fear, it is not an emotion. If you love someone very much, and you fear for that individual in any way, that is not Divine. If you fear inner action in any way, that is not Divine. Any fear at all is emotion. But that is OK. Remember emotions are not bad. They are just part of the ego system. When you are experiencing an unconditional flow (such as joy), without fear, then joy is there regardless of what is going on in your life. If instead, you are experiencing the emotions (such as happiness), the emotion will usually be dependent upon the event, the person or item. Joy is not happiness. Happiness is an emotion, and therefore always dependent upon the creations of the ego. Joy has no fear and has nothing to do with the chakras. Joy is Divinity and a spiritual state of being.

Q: *Can you be concerned without being in fear?*

A: Can you love and feel for the life of someone, being concerned, supporting, praying, holding the person in light and have no fear for what will happen to the person? This is your first step, for indeed you can, and is the difference between concern and fear. If you are afraid of the result of something, that is fear. But if your concern leads to giving support without the fear of what the result will be, you have taken a step away from fear. If you take this step, the result is much more likely to be what you desire because fear only feeds energy to what you are afraid will take place.

Q: *I have tried my whole life to be good. I know from my church teachings being angry is sinful. I am having a lot of trouble at this time in my life with anger. I am working on forgiveness and someone very wise said love is forgiving. I am wondering if the emotional chakra might be the doorway to forgiveness?*

A: Forgiveness has more to do with the heart chakra than the emotional chakra. But let me address the emotional chakra aspects of your question.

Your belief is that you are your ego system. Your ego system is primarily controlled by your emotions and designed to determine if you are safe or not in any circumstance. Anger certainly is a very intense emotion, and I do not know why humanity feels anger will promote safety, but certainly it seems anger might frighten anything threatening your safety. Anger is a paper tiger having no teeth, no power, and punches in the air. But anger does shatter vibrations, scatters creativity, and it will destroy bridges built between Love and humanity.

The only real power is Love. The more you rely on the fear-based emotions of the ego, the more they will entrap you and the more helpless you will feel. You will feel dependent upon those paper tigers, whatever they may be, to keep you safe, and they cannot do it. Recognize anger for what it is, and if you are angry, honor the anger. We are not saying to never be angry, or to bury it, or to act as if it is not there. We are saying to honor wherever you are at and recognize why you are there, what the purpose is, and how it serves you. What is anger doing for you in your life, how is it benefiting you and how is it constructive to you becoming more at peace and in harmony with yourself and all of life on the planet?

The only reality is Love, and that is not the emotion of love, for the emotion of love is also fear-based. Love is the reality of the power that you are. The more you allow yourself to clear the fear-based emotions, the more the power of love comes through and anger dissipates. There just is not a reason for anger because you are so strong in your own center; you do not have a need for a defense. You do not have the need to protect yourself by emotional outbursts of frustration, depression, or whatever. It is only the external that can flare up the emotions, and when you are centered and safe, then the external cannot touch that. Love goes beyond the ego to the truth, the center, and the real power of who you are. When you reach that stage, you do not have to worry about anger or other emotions.

You see anger is survival. You think, "If I do not get angry, I will be a doormat, and people will walk over me. I, therefore, have to do something that says you have to recognize I am a person that is to be valued, and if not, I will make you value me; I will make you aware I am a person." All of this is ego, pain, and struggle.

We would like to suggest there is something within you that is much, much more. Within you is a power far beyond those interactions of pain, and of validation. You play such games in your ego system for validation to say I exist and

emotions are a big part of the game. The only way the emotions bring joy, peace, harmony, and Love is when you center
and allow Love to flow through the emotional field. It is a
process you have to trust, allow, and feel safe enough to begin to move to that point. You will not be vulnerable when
you move into your space of real power, for you will have a
strength that will not attract the things to make you angry.

Humanity does not want to live in fear and therefore is
trying to heal. Over and over you create the experiences giving you the opportunities to heal. When you move into the
place of power, you do not draw those experiences to you. It
is a whole, different world. There is no way to describe this
different world to you because the ego and the mind are totally separate from that understanding. So you have to move
into a place of trust, belief, and allowance.

Questions – Heart Chakra

Q: *What is the connection between the heart chakra and the
soul?*

A: The soul is the individualized expression of the Spirit.
Spirit is all one; it is the God essence of life. Your soul is how
you have taken that Spirit-created ability and used it in your
individual expression. Therefore, the soul and the expression
of your reality residing in the heart chakra are tightly connected.

Now Spirit is more than energy. Energy is as fine as you
know how to define existence, and Spirit is even finer than
energy. From Spirit comes the soul, and the soul vibration
contains the seeds of Spirit. The heart chakra of love, which

also contains the essence of your expression or the Spirit, and therefore unites and aligns very closely with the soul.

Q: *What is the difference between emotional love and unconditional love?*

A: The unconditional love of who you are is a given and is always there. It is the expression of the emotion of love that has blocked the heart chakra. The heart chakra is the center for the emotion of love. But because of the integration of the soul within the heart chakra, there is always the reality of unconditional love. As you remove the blockages within the heart chakra, you allow more of the unconditional love to be a part of who you are in your expression, and your emotion of love will have a different tenor to it.

Q: *If you were to give the first chakra a negative (not in the bad sense) and give the crown chakra a positive, where does this place the heart chakra?*

A: I feel you are speaking of the polarity of physical survival versus spirituality. I would say that is not the way to do it. It has been tried many times. But it does not work that way because you are not two separate beings, one being physical and the other spiritual. You need to flow in harmony and balance and that comes from the spiritual essence.

The spiritual essence knows perfectly and exactly what is required to heal each center and to have it function in harmony connected to the physical existence you desire. The connection to the Earth will be based in Love. The heart chakra sets in the center of the physical and spiritual, but what is that but ego and reality? We have already stated that both experience and expression are contained in the heart chakra. What you want to do instead of attempting to pull the spiritual essence into the heart is to open up and allow the spiritual essence to flow through the heart. As you allow the flow, you are going to express. To express in the physical is much different from experiencing through the ego in the physical. It is a whole, different existence on the planet.

Q: *How do you love someone who does not love one's self?*

A: First I would ask why is it necessary for someone to Love one's self to Love the person? It is not a prerequisite for a person to Love one's self in order to Love the person. All you need to do is embrace the person, as the person is, and not in your perception of what the person should be. For you see, we could say, "You do not Love yourself, and therefore we cannot Love you." But because you do not recognize your beauty and your light has nothing to do with us recognizing your beauty and light. So even if a person does not recognize the beauty, the light, and the Love the person is, that has nothing to do with you seeing it within the person.

In fact, by you seeing the Love within the person will help the person to see the Love within him or herself. For you see, what you see in another does affect the person. By constantly seeing the shortcomings, the faults, and the irritants of another only enhance that vibration within the person. But if you by-pass all of that and say, "I see only the Love and light in you. I do not see all the trappings that you have put on this costume. It does not matter if you have a torn sleeve and one is shorter than the other or it does not match, I only see the Divinity in you and that is no different than the Divinity in me." So if you can by-pass the fear of the ego, moving instead into the expression of Love, allowing Love to come forth and permeate the person then without saying a word the vibration will change. You will change the vibration for yourself and you will help another person to free themselves from their fears.

Questions – Throat Chakra

Q: *Is it important that we sing?*

A: Sound is your only true expression on this planet. You can say the word yes, yes, yes which is a force that will bring about a manifestation. Sound is a creative power, and when you sing, you increase the vibration of your sound because it comes from more sound ranges. Singing brings a joy to the words and brings your expressive power into your sound. Singing is an expression.

Q: *Is it the same with music?*

A: Music comes from the universe and is combined within the physical forming a sound vibration. And of course, sound is expression being naturally aligned with your throat chakra. Music, words, and sound are very powerful forms of expression. This is why you should watch your words and thoughts. It is important to say what you want instead of complaining about what you do not want.

Questions – Third-Eye Chakra

Q: *Is seeing visions during meditations linked at all to the third-eye chakra or any of the major chakras?*

A: There is no question that visions are linked to the third-eye chakra. It might be interesting to discuss one day how you have substituted imagination for the third-eye. A part of you recognizes the great power of your third-eye and so the ego substituted imagination for it. If you can imagine it, you can create it, and this is true in the ego system. But that is like operating with a little drip of water when you could have the whole faucet turned on. So when you ask about visions, if they are true visions, they will go beyond imagination and project from the spiritual essence that comes forth. It is not because you have constructed it, you see.

Q: *Is the third-eye chakra associated with the pineal gland in the brain?*

A: First let us go to vibrational patterns. The vibrational patterns create what you perceive as solid third-dimensional forms or reflections of various areas of the vibrational patterns. Some of those reflections you have committed to understanding, or have an attachment or desire to those vibrational patterns. The pineal gland is one of those and sinus is another. There are other areas as well, but we prefer to stay with the vibrational pattern itself rather than dealing with the reflections, for the vibrational pattern is the true you. Reflections are working with the effect, and we want to work with the source. So we like to work with the vibrational pattern.

The short answer to your question is yes; it is associated.

Q: *Say the mind does not think for itself, it just connects to the oneness of life and all of the thoughts that exist. The mind just receives the thoughts like a radio. Is that true of the mind, and is the third-eye in direct connection to the Divine mind?*

A: Your analytical mind is only a data processing center so it brings in stimuli from many areas whether that is the mass consciousness, beyond your universe, somebody sending you a thought, or something seen or heard. The mind takes in all the data and processes it so it can give you an analysis. Now the third-eye by-passes all of the analytical ego processes, for the original source of the third-eye is not connected at all to the analytical ego processes but comes from All-That-Is, from Divinity. The third-eye deals with reality not with your perceptions or your illusion. The third-eye is the Divine essence and therefore connected to the Divine mind.

Questions – Crown/Spiritual Chakra

Q: *After we leave our physical bodies and attain the possibility of light bodies, do the chakras go with us at that time?*

A: The chakras are always a part of your vibrational pattern relative to the physical universe.

Questions - Working With The Chakras

Q: *Is the technique of clearing the chakras better by visual-*

izing the pathways or is it the intent to clear these perceptions?

A: Visualizing the pathways can be beneficial and effective if you are comfortable with that process. It certainly does not negate from the clearing process, but to visualize does not happen without the intent to visualize. Likewise, without the intent to clear your chakras the clearing process cannot be activated. Therefore, setting your intent to clear the chakras is key. The intent to clear automatically takes your vibration into the Energy Pathways. It is really so simple. You do not have to work at it. We have done the work for you in clearing the Energy Pathways. These Energy Pathways have been given to you, and your intent will take you there. The pathways were given as an act of Love and because you are ready for the experience. How you use the pathways is up to you. Do not make it hard on yourself. Do not make anything hard on yourself. Have fun and play with the process.

Q: *If I clear the chakras for a week, will I pretty much have cleared everything out of my chakras?*

A: I wish I could say that is so but I cannot. As much as you allow the clearing to take place within yourself recognize it is an ongoing process. Remember you are still processing experiences and forming perceptions that are coming back into the chakras. But the clearer the chakras become the easier it is to keep them clear because you are not dealing with the same multitude of fears. Therefore, you are going to be lighter and feel safer, but clearing the chakras is an ongoing process at least for now in the evolution of your consciousness.

Q: *If I wish to connect to the pathways for the whole day, does it take a steady consciousness to hold the connection?*

A: The pathways will disconnect at the point your attention leaves because you see it is a matter of freewill. Therefore, if you are not expressively focusing upon that intent, the pathways will disconnect.

If you desire the pathways stay connected all day, I would suggest you do not plan other activities for the day. You see many things are shifting in your vibrational pattern when you are clearing the chakras. I would not suggest you connect the pathways with the intent to be there for prolonged periods of time such as all day. The human psyche is truly not equipped to deal with such a rapid amount of change.

Q: *Is there a healthy balance?*

A: Nothing says that if you are feeling a little out of center, you cannot take a few moments and connect to the pathways with your intent of clearing, thanking your chakras and the the universe for the clearing, then disconnect. It does not have to be a long ritual to clear the chakras. But I do not think you are ready to be in that constant alignment all day.

Q: *Is it possible to experience pain as the blockages are released from the chakras?*

A: If you resist the release, there could be pain. You think you want to let go of things, but there is a part of you that is not very comfortable with releasing what you have known. What you have known is like a fortress you have very carefully built one brick at a time to keep you safe, and now you are tearing it down. If there is fear or resistance to that, you will not feel safe, and you will create more pain in order to build the fortress again. So you need to reassure the ego, the mind, and your consciousness that your Divine essence is perfectly capable of protecting and keeping you safe within the physical.

Q: *Why should I not feel threatened? Is it not beneficial to determine that I may be unsafe in certain situations?*

A: Your safety is never threatened. You cannot be unsafe. It is only your perceptions that conclude you can be unsafe or threatened. You cannot be destroyed.

The chakras serve the purpose of letting the Divine mind flow through your vibrational pattern. Blockages in the chakras prevent this. So there are two effects of chakra blockages: one is to prevent or distort the flow of Divine energy through your vibrational pattern, and the other is a source of limiting or distorting information through your perceptions that cause you to limit yourself. The first effect is more predominant in the upper three chakras, and the second effect is more predominant in the lower three chakras.

Q: *Some people have written about an eighth chakra at the base of the skull. How true and accurate is this information?*

A: Information coming to the planet is often given at a level of understanding that is in alignment with the thought processes at the time.

Consider yourself a vibrational pattern. You are not in touch with or have the awareness of many things within this vibrational pattern. I suspect the information you are talking about is attempting to say your vibration is increasing enough, at least for some, that you are becoming aware of other sources within your vibrational pattern. The more spiritually aware and aligned you become, the more connected and in tune you become with who you are. Now who you are, is truly a spiritual being.

When you ask is there an eighth chakra, there are more chakras than the seven major chakras. There are minor chakras that flow into the major chakras and there are more major chakras than the seven that have been mentioned. But the other major chakras for the most part have not functioned for so long, they are dormant and have no awareness of their existences. They are almost like an organ you can live without—such as an appendix. So there is much clearing to do.

Glossary

A

Affirmation   An affirming or confirming ratification or declaration. Affirmations are useful in helping to change the perceptions of thought patterns thereby allowing transformation to begin. Affirmations are beneficial in planting and forming new and differing beliefs because they affect the mental body and the perceptions by bringing new thoughts to be considered by the subconscious level of the mind. Through this process, affirmations can allow possibilities of existence not previously allowed.

All-Possibilities   Unlimited Possibilities. Every possibility that has ever existed and will ever exist and more.

All-That-Is   Everything that is: God.

Allow   Permitting or letting without obstruction or resistance.

Analytical Mind   The mind associated with the ego portion of the self that believes in limitation and the inherent unsafe nature of existence. The analytical mind is used to calculate safety based on the perceptions of experience and is focused and used to handle physical world tasks.

Ascended Master   One who has been born into the physical, third-dimensional reality and has either evolved beyond or not succumbed to the limitation of the ego belief system. Well-known ascended masters are Jesus and Buddha.

Attachment   An Ego System behavior whereby outcome is attempted to be controlled at the expense of freedom. A fear-based control mechanism. A bond to an experience that is of the ego. A need.

Aura   A subtle, invisible or ethereal emanation having a distinctive but intangible quality surrounding a person or thing. A subtle, intangible energy or vibrational field around the physical body encompassing the mental and emotional bodies.

B

Base Chakra   The first chakra or energy center located at the base of the spine containing the perceptions of everything that has threatened one's survival on the planet during any lifetime. The base chakra grounds you to the Earth.

Being   To exist as existence itself. To know there is no limitation and that you are God. Totally, completely, in one's power without any limitation, drains of energy, interference by other energies, distortions, fear, perceptions, or conceptions; a state of complete power where all things are possible.

Belief   All things that one has come to accept whether that is an opinion, perception, or a revelation. The ego's view of what is.

Belief System   Totality of all beliefs determining the ego's view of the world.

Body   A component of the Vibrational Pattern containing similar and distinct characteristics. The components can be tangible (the physical body) or intangible (the mental and emotional bodies). The intangible bodies (mental and emotional) are described as layers surrounding the tangible (physical) body within the aura.

C

Chakra   A center where consciousness resides governing various attributes of physical and spiritual aspects. An aspect of consciousness created to define experiences and allow expression in the physical, later adapted to also store the perceptions of experiences. Also referred to as an energy center, vortex or wheel of spinning energy.

Chakra System   The collection and interrelation of energy centers or chakras making up the subtle body. Each chakra relates to different areas of the body and consciousness.

Choice   Sorting out, making a decision, determine. Choice is activated by intent.

Collective Consciousness   See **Mass Consciousness.**

Conditional love   The emotion of love that is part of the ego system. Love that will only be given as long as conditions are met and will only be accepted when conditions are met. Love that is contingent upon being safe.

Create   Setting energy into motion from thought.

Creation   Energy set into motion. A vibration.

Creation Process   The process of affecting energy with thought thereby setting energy into motion resulting in a vibration or creation.

Creator   God, Universal Intelligence, Universal Principle. A consciousness that thinks, thus placing energy into motion.

Creative Principle   Divine characteristic of existence. The ability to create and expand and know oneself as an inherent characteristic of existence.

Crown Chakra   The seventh chakra is a spiritual gateway connecting to what is. The Crown chakra is not totally within the body, instead, it can be thought of as a gateway extending from the crown of the head connecting to the spiritual essence. The connection to the higher parts of the self, the angels, the Love of the universe and the higher power where Divinity is focused.

D

Desire   A positive motivator to action. A motivator that pushes one forward, expands one's world without need, or dependence on anything. Desires usually flow in harmony because they are of the soul.

Detachment Not giving your power to the things you do not desire by focusing and attempting to control and manipulate them, whether that is the outcome of events, situations or the behaviors of another. Not having a "need" for something.

Dimension State of consciousness or awareness.

Discernment Perceiving differences without placing a judgment or value system on the differences. Discernment does not empower limitation.

Divine Mind The mind that knows no limit, all possibilities, and that Love is the only reality. The source of eternal consciousness. The Spirit, All-That-Is, connected to the soul. The part of the self that is all-possibilities, has awareness of everything that is, and is the totality of the expressive experience of the soul's journey.

Divinity The quality or condition given or inspired by God.

E

Ego The part of the self that directly interfaces with physical reality. The ego is the exterior portion of the self that is thought of as one's self. Typically the ego views existence through the limited perception and fear-based opinions of who you are. In the broadest sense, the ego is not compelled to view existence from a limited perception but is simply a portion of the self viewing experience.

Ego Belief System   A belief system based on the separation of the self from the Creative Source. The belief that you are not a creator and things are fixed and unchangeable.

Ego System   A system devised by the self in order to keep the self safe. The emotions and analytical mind are parts of the ego system. The emotions are the first line of defense that react to perceived safety issues. The analytical mind is used to calculate safety based on past experiences. The ego system lives from the perceptions of experiences.

Embrace   To take in one's heart and love unconditionally.

Emotional Body   The intangible outermost body within the aura comprised of the emotions as the first line of defense for the ego system. The emotional body is situated within the aura so that all vibrations must first come through this body to determine one's safety.

Emotional Chakra   The third chakra located along the spine in the area of the solar plexus containing the perceptions of the emotions.

Emotional Love   An emotion of the ego system based on conditions and fear. Emotional love loves as long as it is safe and conditions are met. Emotional love also accepts love only when conditions are met. Love based in fear: fear of rejection, fear of losing a loved one. The emotion of love will always be conditioned upon the perception of survival.

Emotions Part of the ego system. First line of defense when the ego feels threatened or unsafe. Anger, frustration, sadness and the emotion of love are examples of emotions. Emotions are reactionary and based in fear

Energy The raw component of existence, containing all-possibilities, from which all things are created. Energy is the self-expression of All-That-Is, God.

Energy Center See **Chakra**

Energy-In-Motion See **Creation**

Energy Pathways Clear, undistorted fields of intent, allowing limiting perceptions and blockages within the chakras to easily move into Love for healing and transformation. The Energy Pathways are anchored and maintained by beings of Love for the benefit of humanity.

Energy Pattern See **Vibrational Pattern**

Expanding Consciousness Expand awareness going beyond the reality and possibilities of current everyday experience.

Etheric The vibrational pattern in motion but not in a tangible form. The latent possibilities, the image, and the framework from which all human creation begins. Vibration that is the Spiritual Divinity of existence sustaining life in the physical.

Existence Creation in motion. A state of becoming, changing, transforming, and expanding.

Experience Everything the conscious mind is aware of within an event or a happening.

Expression To experience without limitation. Living in the fullness of an experience without judgment, attachments, or needs, and in the fullness of the now-moment. Living in a state of peace, harmony, bliss or joy. Experiencing outside of the emotions and the ego, from a state of the totality that you are.

F

Fear Anything limiting you in any way whether threatening or non-threatening. Anything that limits you from expressing and being the power you are through the Love you are. The absence of Love: the absence of the reality of Love of who you are. A result of the ego belief system.

Feelings Not reactionary (as opposed to emotions). Feelings verify existence as in "feeling alive." Spiritual beings express through feeling their existences i.e. your power, beauty, life expression. Aliveness, vibrant.

Flow The result of power; existence without struggle or resistance to what is.

G

God Total self-aware, intelligent consciousness that contains all-possibilities. Universal Total Intelligence that became self-aware and thought. Universal Self-Aware Principle. The individualized understanding of All-That-Is.

God Essence The essence of God: Spirit.

H

Harmony Acceptance of all things as they are without the need to control, manipulate or change what is; an innate state of Being, a spiritual state.

Healing Bringing one's self, the body, or emotions into a state of harmony with life; a state that reflects Divinity rather than the pain of the ego.

Heart Chakra The fourth chakra located along the spine in the area of the heart containing the perceptions of love on the level of the emotions and on the level of spirituality. The energies of the lower three chakras and upper three chakras connected in the center of love within the heart chakra. The heart chakra is the connection between physical and spiritual allowing the two to manifest.

Higher Self Portions of the self beyond the ego. Soul, spiritual self, and portions of the self connected to the Divine Mind and Spirit.

Honoring   Holding <u>all</u> creations in high regard or great respect. Honoring requires non-judgment. When you honor you take a giant step forward in loving unconditionally.

I

Illusion   A view of the world from the belief that the world as it is known is fixed, must be a certain way, and cannot be changed. Everything the ego system believes is real.

Infinite Intelligence   See **God**

Infinite Possibilities   See **All Possibilities**

Inner Self   The portion of your soul within you. Sometimes referred to as the Human Soul.

Intangible   A vibration (creation) that does not have a shape, form, or reflection associated with it.

Intelligence   The ability to become self-aware, recognize the self-awareness and become coherent in the self-awareness producing a defined result.

Intent   Activator. Intent resonates within the universe activating the creative power and ability to manifest setting energy into a vibrational pattern. To move in a direction without question. Determination in expressing futurity.

J

Joy   A spiritual state. Seeing the beauty in all things. Happiness without dependence on what is happening.

Judgment   Placing a value on one's experience, good/bad, right/wrong. It is impossible to reach the Divine mind if judgments are held

K

Knowing   Truth without reasoning.

L

Limitation Excluding all-possibilities. Not going beyond the known possibilities within the analytical mind.

Love   The unconditional ability to see all things in their Divine order and good. Existing in an eternal state of Being that holds all of life together; God expressing. The Reality. Acceptance and embracing without need, attachment or judgment. Love encompasses peace, harmony, and joy. The true and only reality: an innate state of Being, a spiritual state. Love loves for no other reason other than because it exists. A level of consciousness having the understanding all is in harmony and Divine order. The totality of the soul expressing in every way, every modality, and on every level of consciousness that the soul is choosing to express in its creative existence at this time. Love is the totality of creative existence. All that you are as creation in motion.

Lower Chakras   The lower three chakras: base chakra,

sexual/creativity chakra, and emotional chakra. These chakras together govern the basis of physical existence. Experience is connected with these chakras.

M

Manifesting Bringing a creation into conscious awareness. Thoughts of possibilities coming into existence within the physical dimension. Creations that can be seen within the physical.

Mass Consciousness The collective, conscious awareness of all souls within the physical dimension.

Meditation A centering process whereby the physical mind and body are attuned to its spiritual source.

Mental Body An intangible body within the aura, part of the vibrational pattern made up of the conscious and subconscious mind that is part of the ego system. The mental body will store in an analytical manner the events of experiences, processing data and making decisions with respect to one's safety. See **Analytical Mind.**

Multidimensional Being of more than one dimension or state of consciousness.

N

Need Motivator to action. Motivates an action to control out of fear from the ego.

Non-Judgment Not placing a value on experiences as being good/bad, right/wrong. See **Judgment.**

Now-Moment A state where power is expressed, and creation takes place. Not in the past or future. A state where consciousness has no conception or perception of what existence is, rather is all-possibilities, unlimited.

P

Peace In harmony with everything around one's self. Coming from unconditional love. Spirit is the source of peace; an innate state of Being; a spiritual state.

Perceptions The result of the ego system's analysis of how past experiences or similar experiences have affected one's self. The ego's basis for evaluation of existence.

Physical Body The tangible component of the vibrational pattern.

R

Reality Knowing that one is all-possibilities, unlimited with the power to create everything known and more. God expressing; Love

Reflection The result or end product of the creation process. Your response to the perception of a vibration.

Resisting Not accepting what is; attempting to push away.

Trying to rid one's self of an experience or creation by attempting to push away that part of one's self.

Root Chakra   See **Base Chakra**

S

Self   All portions of the soul expressing in a point of consciousness to include the portions that are within the conscious awareness as well as the inner or higher portions supporting the point of consciousness.

Sexual/Creativity Chakra   The second chakra located along the spine in the area of the naval containing the perceptions of sexuality and creativity as it pertains to life (procreation).

Spirit   The characteristics of God within you: the inherited essence of God. The pure essence of omnipotence. Who you are vibrating at the rate that contains all-possibilities. That part that is Divine.

Spiritual Chakra   See Crown Chakra

Spiritual Essence   The characteristics or inherited essence of God contained within all creations whether recognized by the creation or not, allowing forward movement, expression and becoming.

Spiritual States   Innate states of Being not dependent on external events or happenings. Joy, Love, harmony, and peace. Not dependent upon external motivations or stimuli.

State of Consciousness A state of awareness. See **Points of Consciousness.**

Soul The individualized expression of All-That-Is. The individualized consciousness of your Spirit that goes forth from the Creator.

Subconscious The unconscious portion of the self. The holding tank within the mental body that contains the memory of all experiences and thoughts not presently within the conscious mind.

Subtle Body The intangible bodies and chakras making up an individual's vibrational pattern. The mental, emotional bodies and chakras are parts of the subtle anatomy.

Surrender Allowing your soul and Spirit to control your life. Removing barriers between you and whatever is, opening to receive and accept. Letting go of everything.

T

Tangible A vibration that has a shape or form. Opposite of intangible.

The Physical Existence within the physical dimension. See **Third-Dimensional Physical**

Third-Dimension Physical Everything existing on the planet and in your world you consider being physical.

Third-Eye Chakra   The sixth chakra located in the middle of the forehead. When clear, this chakra is used as the source of information as it enters the vibrational pattern from the spiritual essence. This chakra connects to the intuitive, inner knowing—the Spirit. This chakra is about living from knowing instead of understanding. The third-eye chakra acts as an intermediary between the crown chakra and the rest of the vibrational pattern.

Thought   Self-aware intelligence. Vibrating energy pattern.

Throat Chakra   The fifth chakra located along the spine in the area of the throat containing the perceptions of all of one's manifestations. The throat chakra governs the ability to create through expression. It is the center of will and expression.

Trust   Knowing that your soul and Spirit work for your best interest.

Truth   That, that resonates within you, a knowing.

U

Unconditional Love   Love without conditions, simply because it exists. See Love

Universal Mind   Mind of God. See **Divine Mind**.

Upper Chakras   The upper, three chakras consisting of the throat chakra, third-eye chakra, and the crown chakra. Together these three chakras govern the spiritual aspects and connect to the spiritual essence. Expression is connected with these chakras.

V

Value System   Determining if something is good or bad, right or wrong, safe or not safe. Judging.

Vibration   Energy set in motion. All creations are energy (the raw substance of creation) set in motion or vibrate. Energy set in motion forms a creation that vibrates at a particular rate or vibration. Taken in this way Vibration = Energy Set In Motion = Creation. A creation that can be tangible or intangible.

Vibration Pattern   The composite of all of one's creations (or vibrations) forming a unique pattern that is you. Most creations are complex in that they have more than one vibration or creation of which they are made. Whether the creation is simple or complex, the resulting pattern from the vibration(s) is termed a Vibration Pattern or Vibrational Pattern. The Vibrational Pattern is also sometimes referred to as an energy pattern. Your vibrational pattern can be broken down into various components, consisting of your physical, emotional and mental bodies along with a system of chakras.

W

Who You Are   A being of totality that is Love, creative existence. All that you are as creation in motion; Love. See **Love**.

Will   Having strong purpose or determination. The power of conscious and deliberate action or choice.

Index

A

Abandonment 92, 95
Abundance 118
All possibilities 56
All-possibilities 30, 34, 106
All-That-Is
    91, 92, 100, 105, 109, 110,
    115, 143
Analytical mind
    9, 10, 22, 51, 56, 82, 99,
    101, 105, 107, 108, 143
Angels 111, 112, 113, 129
Anger 31, 41, 136
    as survival 137
    scatter creativity 136
    shatter vibrations 136
Ascended masters 129
Aspect of consciousness
    3, 35, 44
Attachment
    17, 100, 101, 109, 122
    future outcome 22
    maintaining safety 18
    need 18
Aura 37, 41, 43, 44
    as a composite energy field
    37
    as energy field 37
    ethereal emanation 37

B

Base chakra. *See* Chakra:
    major: base/survival
Beauty 78, 96, 118
Belief system 51

Bio-energy field. *See* Energy
    field
Blockage 53
    to success in life 52
Blockages
    53, 57, 60, 62, 63, 64, 82,
    87, 96, 110, 115, 133
    as distorted, limiting
        information 146
    distorting flow of energy
    146
Bodies
    etheric 32
    light 40, 143
    physical, mental, emotional
    32, 43, 44, 47, 48, 57, 108
    subtle 37

C

Cellular
    existence 91
    memory 134
Center of
    awareness 4
Love 92, 117
    will & expression 100, 101
Centering 55, 138. *See also*
    Meditation
Chakra
    35, 43, 44, 47, 86. *See*
    also Energy center
    alignment of 56
    center of awareness 4
    center of consciousness 44
    clearing
    49, 53, 55, 61, 61–66,
    68–70, 116, 120, 121,
    122, 143, 144
    energy pathways 60

Clarmar Publishing

A Division of Clarmar LLC

Quick Order Form

Telephone Orders: Call 1-866-877-6992 toll free. Have your credit card ready
Email Orders: orders@PathToRemembrance.com
orders@ClarmarPublishing.com
Postal Orders: Clarmar Publishing, PO. Box 619, Lincolnshire, Illinois, 60069-0619

Please send the following items. I understand that I may return any item for full refund – for any reason, no questions asked.

_____

_____

_____

Please send Free Information on:
___Other books, ___Speaking/ Seminars,___Tapes

Please place me on your Notification List___

Name:_____
Address:_____
City:_____ State:_____Zip Code:_____
Telephone:_____
Email Address:_____

Sales Tax: Please add 7.5% for products shipped to Illinois Addresses.

Shipping - Please add:
U.S.: $4.00 for first book or disk and $2.00 for each additional product.
International: $9.00 for first book or disk; $5.00 for each additional product (estimate).
Payment:___Cheque___MC_____Visa___Discover
Card Number_____
Name on Card _____ Exp. Date_____